Twayne's United States Authors Series

Sylvia E. Bowman, *Editor*

INDIANA UNIVERSITY

Hugh Henry Brackenridge

HUGH HENRY BRACKENRIDGE

By **DANIEL MARDER**

COLLEGE & UNIVERSITY PRESS · *Publishers*

NEW HAVEN, CONN.

FOR
BARBARA HUMPHREY MARDER

Preface

ALTHOUGH Hugh Henry Brackenridge published poetry all his life, his literary strength was in prose. His verse includes a few commencement poems, one in collaboration with Princeton classmate Philip Freneau; two tragic dramas; many satires that he called "Hudibrastics"; and a series of Scottish dialect poems. As a literary man, he was the first to condemn these poetic efforts; but they are no worse than other examples of surviving American poetry of the time. A few dialect poems of recollected boyhood, in fact, are impressive.

The literary reputation of Hugh Henry Brackenridge rests to-day solely on his novel *Modern Chivalry*. Brackenridge is recognized as the writer of the third or fourth American novel; but many of his essays and narratives are works of lasting literary value because of what they say and how they say it. Like the prose of his contemporary, Philip Freneau, most of Brackenridge's writing was stimulated by public affairs. However, like Freneau, he wrote within the disciplines of literary art and for literary effect. The essays and narratives of Brackenridge may have been brushed aside as mere journalism, but they are no more nor less journalistic than Addison's. Journals were the publishing mode of the time both in America and in England, and the high level of work contained in them establishes an equation between the terms *journalistic* and *literary*.

Altogether, his life and works have an esthetic appeal and a significance not fully realized. Brackenridge was an American literary man trying to plant the values of the Enlightenment in the life of the frontier. His work enriches the sparse period of American literary output between the Revolution and the end of the eighteenth century. This study, therefore, attempts to evaluate Brackenridge's life and work in terms of art and history.

The chapters progress through the forces that molded his life and writing to an evaluation of his writing and its place in American literary history. They trace his literary development from the ambitions of an immigrant boy in Pennsylvania's "Barrens" to his classical training at Princeton, through the collision of the ambitious classicist with frontier realities that produced his best work, and finally to his eastward retreat as Supreme Court Justice of Pennsylvania. Although this evaluation concentrates on his best work, it does not neglect his early writing at Princeton, in the army, and for the *United States Magazine,* all dominated by his revolutionary ideals both in government and art. Nor does it neglect his miscellaneous work after his retreat—writings dominated by a wistfulness summoned through the review of his early ideals and the impact of frontier life upon them.

The major works—satires and narratives—are analyzed in terms of thought, style, and mood; and in these terms they are related to the work of his time. The analysis avoids the usual probing for archetypes and symbolic significations. Such efforts would lead the reader completely away from the typically utilitarian intent of Brackenridge. Typical also for late eighteenth-century American literature are the buds of sensibility appearing almost everywhere in the landscape of Brackenridge work. Here and there, in fact, they bloom.

The analysis leads finally to Brackenridge's appropriate place in American literature—a literary pioneer on the early frontier—by revealing the ways in which he is atypical of his times and in which he may prefigure later literary modes such as local color and realism.

DANIEL MARDER

Contents

Chronology

1748   Hugh Henry Brackenridge born in Kintyre, near Campbellstown, Scotland.

1753   Arrives in America with parents, who settle family in the "Barrens" of York County, Pennsylvania.

1755   Lives through Indian terrors in York County following General Braddock's defeat.

1763   Appointed teacher in a free school at Gunpowder Falls, Maryland.

1768   Enters the College of New Jersey, Princeton.

1770   Collaborates with Philip Freneau on "Father Bombo's Pilgrimage to Mecca."

1771   Receives Bachelor of Arts degree; recites "The Rising Glory of America," written in collaboration with Philip Freneau, at commencement exercises.

1772   Becomes master of academy at Back Creek, Somerset County, Maryland.

1774   Visits Annapolis where he is influenced by Attorney Samuel Chase; receives a Master of Arts degree and recites his "Poem on Divine Revelation" at the Princeton commencement exercises.

1775   Writes first drama, *The Battle of Bunkers-Hill.*

1776   Joins Washington's army as chaplain; publishes *The Battle of Bunkers-Hill.*

1777   Publishes second drama, *The Death of General Montgomery at the Siege of Quebec;* delivers political sermons to the troops.

1778   Publishes *Six Political Discourses founded on the Scriptures.*

1779   Establishes and edits *United States Magazine;* delivers "An Eulogium of the Brave Men who have fallen in the Contest with Great Britain" at Philadelphia.

1780   Admitted to Philadelphia bar.

1781   Relocates in the frontier village of Pittsburgh; changes middle name from Montgomery to Henry.

1783   Sends first report from the frontier to a newspaper back East, "Narrative of the Perils and Sufferings of Dr. Knight and John Slover."

1784   Visits Warm Springs, Virginia, at the same time President Washington vacations there; composes in Washington's honor, *A Masque, Written at the Warm-Springs in Virginia, in the Year 1784.*

1785   Defends twelve rioters accused of attacking the excise collector, William Graham; also defends Mamachtaga, an Indian charged with the murder of two white men; writes "The Trial of Mamachtaga"; marries a Miss Montgomery.

1786   Helps found first newspaper on the frontier, *The Pittsburgh Gazette;* elected to the State Assembly of Pennsylvania; his son, Hugh Marie, is born May 11.

1787   Obtains state endowment for the Pittsburgh Academy (University of Pittsburgh) and succeeds in passing bills establishing Allegheny County and a church in Pittsburgh; fights for the adoption of the new Federal Constitution; composes his first Hudibrastic satires.

1788   Defeated in re-election effort; begins *Modern Chevalier;* delivers "Oration on the Federal Constitution."

1789   Repudiates Federalist party.

1790   Marries Sofia Wolfe.

1792   Publishes *Modern Chivalry,* Volumes I and II, Philadelphia.

1793   Publishes *Modern Chivalry,* Volume III, Pittsburgh.

1794   Attempts role of mediator in the Whiskey Rebellion.

1795   Publishes *Incidents of the Insurrection in Western Pennsylvania in the Year 1794.*

1796   Writes Scottish dialect poems in response to David Bruce.

1797   Publishes *Modern Chivalry,* Volume IV, Philadelphia.

1798   Returns to political activity; becomes leader of Jefferson's Republican Party in Western Pennsylvania.

1799   Appointed a judge of the Supreme Court of Pennsylvania.

1800   Establishes *Tree of Liberty* in opposition to the *Pittsburgh Gazette*.

1801   Continues writing Scottish poems in response to those of David Bruce; relocates in Carlisle, Pennsylvania.

1804   Defends fellow supreme court judges in impeachment proceedings; publishes *Modern Chivalry*, Part II, Philadelphia, Baltimore, Washington, Pittsburgh, Norfolk, Carlisle.

1806   Collects and publishes *Gazette Publications* and *The Spirit of the Public Journals: or Beauties of American Newspapers, for 1805*.

1807   Begins task of adopting English common law to American society.

1810   Poses for a portrait by Gilbert Stuart.

1811   Visits Pittsburgh, where he writes *An Epistle to Walter Scott*.

1814   Publishes *Law Miscellanies*, Philadelphia.

1815   Republishes *Modern Chivalry*, with additions.

1816   Dies at Carlisle, Pennsylvania, June 25.

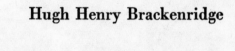

Hugh Henry Brackenridge

CHAPTER 1

The Rising Glory

O N COMMENCEMENT DAY, September 25, 1771, in Nassau Hall, Princeton, the son of a poor Scottish farmer who had immigrated to the "Barrens" of York County in Pennsylvania, delivered the following lines:

> 'Tis but the morning of the world with us
> And Science yet but sheds her orient rays.
> I see the age, the happy age, roll on
> Bright with the splendours of her mid-day beams.
> I see a Homer and a Milton rise
> In all the pomp and majesty of song,
> Which gives immortal vigour to the deeds
> Atchiev'd by Heros in the fields of fame.

Hugh Henry Brackenridge had been selected to give the salutory in the morning and to conclude the program in the afternoon with his poem. "The Rising Glory of America," some 750 lines written with classmate Philip Freneau, was received, according to classmate James Madison, "with great applause by the audience."[1] It was published the next year in Philadelphia. Professor Fred L. Pattee called it the "first real poem that America ever made, the first impelled hot from a man's soul."[2] The poem was epic in scope, as it claims, of "things unattempted yet in prose or rhyme." "The Rising Glory" was early literary fruit of the ideas that forced an American Revolution a few years later; it was an American prophecy.

I *Young Prophet in a New Nation*

Unfortunately, the new nation neglected its young prophets; it was too busy fulfilling their prophecy. According to Professor Pattee, "America should have recognized this new and original voice and should have encouraged it to sing the new message which it had to proclaim to the world, but she was not yet ready." Brackenridge and Freneau had come to maturity at least a generation before young Americans could devote themselves to letters. Like most Americans writing from 1700 through the end of the century, their future work would be concerned with public affairs; but neither young man completely succumbed to necessity. Freneau, who roamed the Atlantic and then settled in the East, aroused the unlettered with the spirit of "Rising Glory" expressed in journalistic veins. Piquing Washington and Hamilton, he earned the reputation of "that rascal." Yet he also created "The Beauties of Vera Cruz," "The British Prison Ship," and "The House of Night"—enduring American verse for which he is often called "the first American poet."

Brackenridge also attempted to stay in the East. At the Princeton commencement in 1774, he read his "Poem on the Divine Revelation," once again showing the destiny of America, the rising glory of the Western world. As an army chaplain, he aroused the troops in the field with political sermons full of reasoned hatred for British and American Tories and of hope for the rising glory. While the colonies were still fighting to become a nation, he established the *United States Magazine* to foster an independent national literature; but America "was not yet ready." Brackenridge blamed the failure of the periodical on that large class who "inhabit the region of stupidity, and cannot bear to have the tranquility of their repose disturbed by the villainous jargon of a book."[3]

He studied law, then turned to the West to seek a career where he had prophesied the rising glory would be fulfilled. When he moved to the frontier settlement that had grown about Fort Pitt, he found no books, no school, no church, no literary men. In this cultural void, the new democracy burgeoned without the traditional fetters and distinctions of the East. Among the crude and the unschooled, it was most apparent to Brackenridge that the success of the democratic experiment depended upon an educated citizenry. To education, to culture, and to the spirit of the rising glory in the new democracy he now devoted his literary and political energies; and upon these ideas he gambled his career. He encouraged two printers from Philadelphia to establish a newspaper and became its most prolific contributor; he persuaded a cousin to stock a bookstore and found a lending library; he aroused public desire for a Pittsburgh academy and sponsored a bill for its founding in the State Assembly (1787); he induced a clergyman to settle and form a congregation in the frontier village, though he himself was not a worshipper; and he spoke and wrote voluminously.[4]

II *The New Audience*

If the writers in the East had little opportunity for belletristic efforts, Brackenridge had even less on the frontier. The tenor of thought in the eighteenth century was political and social. This age of transition from monarchy to democracy had enlarged the literate audience to include the mass of men; and it had brought forth in England, as well as in America, a stream of utilitarian literature. In England, both Whig and Tory feared the lowering of literary standards; their attacks on the Grub Street hacks vividly reflect the change to utilitarian writing for mass taste.

Jonathan Swift, as well as Joseph Addison, turned to the new audience. Swift satirized the contemporary political and social developments with the simplicity, concision, and force that became a model of writing for the new audience. In *A Tale of A Tub* Swift contended that surface knowledge is preferable to "that pretended philosophy which enters the depth of things and then comes gravely back with information and discoveries, that in the inside are good for nothing" (Section LX). In satires, sermons, and political tracts, Swift took care to follow his own precepts: no display of learning or oratory or politeness clouds the immediate effect he seeks. Knowledge, he held, is to be used; it is not intended for idle curiosity or for speculative pleasures.

Addison attempted to assume high literary standards for the new readers while introducing them to John Locke and Robert Boyle (*Spectator* 94), the pleasures of astronomy (*Spectator* 565), and natural history (*Spectator* 120)—all in the same comfortable style he used to distinguish between false and true wit (*Spectator* 70). Addison's appeal to the new audience is reflected most obviously in *Spectator* 70 in which he claims that true poetry "pleases all kinds of palates" but that the false pleases "only such as have formed to themselves a wrong artificial taste upon little fanciful authors." Most guilty of such artificial tastes were the Tories. Addison felt they despised natural science and all the past outside their favorite periods.

But Addison's words apply not only to the Tory poets of England; they apply also to their American imitators, mature men who were still attempting American epics more than a decade after "Rising Glory" and were scribbling satires in the modes of Alexander Pope and Samuel Butler. Brackenridge was not an exception, but he had no illusions that his versification of prosaic thought bore any resemblance to that fusing of elements recognized as poetry. His Hudibrastics were satirical reports, exposés, and attacks intended to inform "Tom, Dick, and Harry in the woods"[5] and to arouse their reactions against the opportunistic demagogues whom they had elected to public office:

> Whence comes it that a thing like this,
> Of mind no bigger than a fly's
> Should yet attract the popular favor,
> Be of his country's thought the savior,
> Sent to assembly and convention
> With votes almost without dissention.[6]

Although Brackenridge won an initial election to the State Assembly in 1786, he experienced a continuous string of political defeats thereafter, testifying to the effect of these Hudibrastics on the frontiersmen.

Even for those few Western families who maintained the Eastern concept of paternalism, the realities of frontier democracy demanded communication without conscious esthetic effort. The Eastern audience was still tied to literary England. Though polite literature was not quite acceptable, verse satire was useful. America, as a whole, could devote no time to anything not useful; but on the Western side of the Alleghenies, even the most popular of satires, such as John Trumbull's *M'Fingal* (1782), represented the artificiality of an effete society.

Despite Brackenridge's efforts to imbue Western audiences with the spirit of "Rising Glory" and to ascend with it, he looked upon himself as a solitary figure. "It is a good deal owing to my solitary residence in the Western country," he tells us, "at a distance from books and literary conversation that I have been led to write at all."[7] His first and only election to the State Assembly in Philadelphia (1786) was most pleasing because he could be "amongst political and literary men for a while." After one term, he returned to his residence in Pittsburgh until he was appointed a justice of the Pennsylvania Supreme Court fifteen years later, as a reward for leading the Jeffersonian party in the Western country.

III *A Portrait of the Early Frontier*

Embroiled all these years in the turbulent politics of frontier democracy, the ardent lover of culture mellowed; the spirit of "Rising Glory" found new expression in forms, moods, and thoughts that reflected the life of the new country far from English dominance. His sermons, orations, essays, narratives, poems, and fiction all congeal into a rare portrait of the spawning democracy. With humor, he brushed in the village gossips, duelers, traders, Scotch-Irish settlers, bogtrotters, and gamblers; with gentle irreverence, the love of whiskey and religion; with invective and satire, the blackguard journalists, the demagogues, the want of education, and the confusion of national ideals; with dramatic intensity, the men and events of the Whiskey Rebellion (1794); with nostalgia, the need of a Western Walter Scott to mirror the American dream in the beauty of the wilderness; with outrage, the Indian atrocities; with pathos, an Indian murderer hanged by the bewildering white man's law. It seems that his pen was always busy. Though he dreamed of creating literary masterworks, he realized his shortcomings. He intended no grand-scale canvas; nonetheless, viewed wholly and steadily, the portrait he has left offers a broad reflection and penetrating criticism of amorphous America.

From a historical viewpoint, the vigorous expression of this portrait comprises data of the frontier activity that molded much of the American spirit; or, in Professor Parrington's words, "a vast drama . . . enacted . . . by players unconscious of their parts. . . . Today it is plain that those unremembered years were engaged in clearing away encumberances more significant than the great oaks and maples of the Virgin wilderness; they were uprooting ancient habits of thought, destroying social customs that had grown old and dignified in class-ridden Europe."[8] At least one player was conscious, and his works also shape his own portrait. They render an image of a unique man, a cultural pio-

[21]

neer, engrossed in a struggle against the ignorance and licentiousness of a newly freed people. According to the *Literary History of the United States,* "While the lady novelists were dispensing simple, serious lessons in morality for young folks, Brackenridge was teaching his fellow men how to be good citizens. His was the harder task. To it he brought not only the wisdom of observation, but also his wide reading from Plato to Swift."[9]

CHAPTER 2

Poet, Preacher, Publisher

IN ONE SENSE OR ANOTHER, the destiny portrayed in "The Rising Glory of America" had been a European dream centuries before the poem was recited at Nassau Hall in 1771. Perhaps its first utterance was Sir Thomas More's *Utopia,* a country set on American shores. In the seventeenth century, the Puritans found on these shores a haven in which they could raise the glory of their theocracy. In the eighteenth century, the dream was nourished by Jean Jacques Rousseau's "natural man," who realized in the new world wilderness a measure of happiness never achieved by civilized man in the old world, and by Voltaire's "civilized man" who found opportunity for a new golden age in William Penn's republic.

In *The Sage and the Atheist,* Voltaire has an American Indian extol Penn: "May the Penns live forever. The great Penn is our Manitou, our god. He and his were the only Europeans who did not deceive us, and seize on our land. He bought the territory we gave up to him; he paid for it liberally; he maintained peace amongst us; he brought us remedies for the few diseases we had caught from the Europeans. He taught us new arts." Voltaire may have been influenced by William Penn's pamphlets issued in several languages to induce migration. These glowing advertisements appealed to the persecuted and to the financially unfortunate of France, of the Lowlands, and of England, Ireland, and Scotland. They offered an opportunity for new fortunes in the Pennsylvania commonwealth.

I   *"The Barrens" and Princeton*

In 1753, a Scottish farmer, impoverished by the civil wars, relinquished his struggles with the land surrounding Campbellstown and sailed with his wife and five-year-old son to Penn's new world. Reaching Philadelphia, William Breckenridge (Hugh

Henry changed it to Brackenridge "because I found the bulk of
the same stock spelt it so.")[1] paid his family's passage with the
sale of surplus clothing; then he continued west to lease some
of the cheap frontier forest of York County, suggestively called
"the Barrens" by the Scotch-Irish immigrants who had settled
there.[2] According to one account, the family walked most of the
way from Philadelphia to York. In a dialect poem recalling his
boyhood, Brackenridge indicated the continuing struggle for
existence in the Barrens:

> And grubbing up the trees, and bleering,
> And burning brush and making fences
> That scares these things out o' their senses;
> And drives them frae our fields and patches.[3]

The "things" are "Dryads, Hamadryads, Muses." But there were
more solid bodies to fear. Indians constantly threatened the men
who hewed the hardwood trees to make their "fields and
patches." For months following General Braddock's defeat of
1755, the Indians terrorized the settlements in these fields; these
events may well have been the source of Brackenridge's fierce
hatred of the native American.

Though the Barrens seemed the least likely environment in
which to cultivate a scholar, it *was* a Scottish settlement. Among
the educated Scots, Latin had been almost as familiar as the
mother tongue. It was the means of communicating with the non-
Scottish world. According to Henry Marie Brackenridge, Hugh
Henry's son, "Like the Scotch in general, William Breckenridge
neglected no opportunity in his power of giving the best education to his children."[4] Nor did the boy Hugh overlook opportunity. In return for Saturday chores, a clergyman taught him
Greek and Latin. At the country school, the teacher complained
that Brackenridge's aptitude for learning "discouraged . . . other
scholars. The pursuit of learning . . . became a passion in which
he manifested that intense ardor and perseverance which charac-
terized him through life." This passion did not release him from
the plough. He recalled:

> When of an age to ca' the plough,
> My father use to say, "Gae Houch,
> And louse the horses frae the tether,
> It's time to yoke.

Then, after dusk, in "the dim light made by chips and splinters, he conned over his book, or books; for he rather devoured than studied them in the ordinary way." A prized possession was his volume of Horace. He suffered the keenest distress the day he left it on a tree stump and returned to find that a "literary cow" had chewed it. His mother, delighted by his intellectual pursuits, anticipated his future as a minister of the gospel.

At fifteen, Hugh presented himself as a teacher to the trustees of the free school at Gunpowder Falls, Maryland, who "were not less surprised at the application than by the qualifications of the applicant, and after some hesitation gave him the place." The young master confirmed his authority the first time a rough lad (some were larger and older) defied it. He "seized a brand from the fire, knocked the rebel down, and spread terror around him." Three years later, when all sources of learning at Gunpowder Falls had been exhausted, he applied to the College of New Jersey (Princeton) and offered to teach grammar school classes in exchange for his college expenses.

The college at Princeton was founded to train students for the Presbyterian ministry, but it was not under church control. Its 1746 charter states that "every religious denomination may have free and equal liberty and advantage of education." Here, the new democratic idealism was astir. Dr. John Witherspoon lectured on the most modern Whig political philosophies. The purpose of a government, he taught, "should be the protection of liberty as far as it is a blessing."[5] Brackenridge immersed himself in the political ideas that were to dominate his life and thought; and from the curriculum he deepened his love of the classics which moderated his idealism, crystallized his satirical manner, and strengthened his zeal and skill for oratory. In the first year he studied Horace, Cicero, Lucian, Xenophon, logic, geography, English grammar and composition, and prepared declamations five nights each week. In the second year his subjects were Homer, Longinus, and mathematics; and he gave declamations five nights each week. The third year he devoted himself to mathematics, natural philosophy, moral philosophy, metaphysics, history, English grammar, eloquence, advanced composition, criticism, and style; and he gave a weekly public declamation and disputation. The final year he studied history, ethics, politics, government, eloquence, and Hebrew and French as electives.

[25]

Throughout his life, the classics remained the spring of his thought: "I converse [he said in *Modern Chivalry*] with the schools of wise men, and solace myself with the company of heroes. . . ." In middle years he forgot most of his later learning but recollected "chiefly my academic studies. Hence it is that the classics are more in my head than Shakespeare, or Milton." Of all the classical authors, Lucian, the Greek satirist, most directly influenced the young scholar's personality. "In the course of my academical studies, I had contracted some taste, and even habit this way [satirical], owing to my reading the dialogues of Lucian in the original Greek. Had I read them in translation, they might have made less impression. But by means of a difficult language, studying them slowly, the turn of thought became more deeply impressed upon my mind." Later, this satirical habit was fortified by "acquaintance with the modern wits, such as Cervantes, LeSage and especially Swift. I found myself still more inclined to an ironical, ludicrous way of thinking and writing."

At Princeton the ironical, ludicrous way was exercised frequently. With Philip Freneau, James Madison, and William Bradford, Brackenridge formed a Whig literary club to oppose the Tories who had united as the Cliosophic Society. A paper war ensued; wits clashed in juvenile satires full of the type of foolery still found in college humor magazines. The literary remains of the conflict, *Satires Against the Tories, Written in the last War between the Whigs and Cliosophians in which the former obtained a complete Victory,* rest among the Bradford Papers at the Historical Society of Pennsylvania. The first ten satires comprise the initial literary efforts of Hugh Henry Brackenridge, and they foretell typical Brackenridge behavior. Satirical verse, as well as fiction, was to become his consistent weapon in the constant stream of disputes that broiled through his life.

In his junior year, Brackenridge collaborated with Freneau to contrive his first fiction. It was a marvelous adventure with the descriptive title "Father Bombo's Pilgrimage to Mecca, wherein is given a true account of the innumerable and surprising adventures which befell him in the course of that long and tedious journey. Till he once more returned safe to his native land, as related by his own mouth. Written by H. B. and P. F. 1770." Only fragments of Volume II are extant in the Bradford Papers.

Book III, Chapter I, is signed by Brackenridge. According to Freneau's biographer, this part is far superior to any of the others;[6] and, according to a Brackenridge biographer, it is "ludicrous and exaggerated" but "deserves attention since it is the earliest example of American prose fiction."[7]

II *Oration and Revelation*

Satirical prose was not then Brackenridge's major channel of expression. Far more significant to him were the solemn orations he prepared for the weekly declamations of his junior year. These required a penetration of classical literature and politics, subjects to which he was most devoted; they also allowed him to exercise his powers of oratorical eloquence. On these glorious occasions, his son recalled, "he stood unequalled. He could reason well, had a fine voice, a fine person, and an eagle eye." Brackenridge's powers of organizing and phrasing allowed him to earn extra income as a ghost writer for fellow students endowed with less talent and more cash. The grateful orator of one well-received piece of Brackenridge eloquence rewarded the ghost writer with a handsome suit and a smartly cocked hat.

Throughout his life Brackenridge relished the opportunity for oratory. This was the aspect of the ministry he found most appealing. Later the chance to exercise these powers influenced his choice of a career in law. Looking back upon his literary achievements, he found consolation in his oratory. He reflected, "Swift said of himself that he could never rise to the stile of an oration or sermon . . . it is not with me as it was with Swift; and in this respect I am his superior; for I can rise to the swell of the highest pipe of diction. And to evince this, I will here produce an oration delivered by me about two years ago. . . ."[8]

In spite of the role he wished to assume in the new America, he remained at Princeton to study for the ministry until he was licensed to preach. Then, instead of a church, he was offered the leadership of an academy on the Eastern shore of Maryland and accepted it at "a handsome salary." According to Freneau, who became his assistant, there were about thirty students in the academy, "who prey upon me like leeches."[9] Brackenridge's attitude, however, was glowing. He delighted in the reputation of the academy. According to his son, the academy was of "considerable eminence" as the leader of "virtue and science" in a "wealthy and highly polished society."

His complacency in teaching and studying was disturbed on a trip to Annapolis, "where for the first time [he writes] I saw Samuel Chace [Chase] with papers in his hand, haranguing the citizens . . . on the Boston port bill," which was not only a cause of Massachusetts but "the cause of America." Brackenridge returned to the academy deeply moved by the "ardent mind, the impressive vigour, the undaunted resolution" of the famous lawyer.[10]

In September, 1774, Brackenridge returned to Princeton for his Master's degree and to read his "Poem on The Divine Revelation," which traced the Christian spirit from Palestine to its ultimate realization in America. Perhaps the image of Samuel Chase haranguing the public conflicted with his religious impulses in creating the poem. At the end of "Divine Revelation" the theme of Christianity has evaporated. Brackenridge speaks of going physically

> Far hence . . . to some sequestered vale
> By woody hill or shady mountain side,
> Where far from converse and the social band,
> My days shall pass inglorious away

and of being buried "on some Western hill." This first reference to the possibility of a life on the Western frontier is also the beginning of his departure from Presbyterian indoctrination. Later, his son reports, "he declared that for two whole years he labored most sincerely and assiduously to convince himself; but in vain and he could not think of publicly maintaining doctrines in which he did not privately believe."

III Heroic Bard

Though parting with piety, Brackenridge clung still to poetry in the grand manner. He responded to the news from Bunker Hill with the drama *Battle of Bunkers-Hill* in which American bravery wrings a moral victory out of defeat. The following year, 1777, on the occasion of the colonists' defeat at Quebec, Brackenridge wrote a second play in the same vein, *The Death of General Montgomery at the Siege of Quebec.*

Both plays were composed in haste and were intended, according to their author, only "for the private entertainment of gentlemen of taste and martial enterprise, but by no means for the exhibition of the stage." Nevertheless, they were written, he added, "according to the prescribed rules of drama, with the strictest attention to the unities of time, place and action." From an account by a French traveler, it appears that both plays were presented at Harvard, and perhaps at other academies. The traveler states: "Their pupils often act tragedies, the subjects of which are generally taken from their national events, such as the battle of Bunker's Hill, the burning of Charleston, the death of General Montgomery. . . ."[11]

These works did not satisfy Brackenridge. "I know myself capable of producing something much better, had I leisure for that purpose," he wrote in the Preface to *General Montgomery;* "but writing in this way is my amusement, not my business." In a businesslike manner, nevertheless, he had hurried his dramas to the press, because ". . . one great foundation of the merit of any performance is its being seasonable. An oration, eulogium or production of any kind in honor of our brave countrymen, who have fallen or of those who do yet contend in the glorious cause of freedom, is likely to do greater good and will be more acceptable at present than hereafter when the foe is entirely repulsed and the danger over." As at Princeton, he was aware of his audience, of the moment, and of the opportunities at hand. Although literary work had become a direct social force to him, he did not yet relinquish the grand manner. In spite of his protest that writing had become his amusement, he did not abandon the literary life as his major occupation; nor had he yet freed himself from the possibility of a clergyman's life.

In 1777, the year in which he completed *The Death of General Montgomery,* Brackenridge gave up teaching to join the troops in the field as an army chaplain. For more than a year, he experienced the life of a soldier in the tent and on the battlefields. He saw the function of chaplain as heroic bard and modern propagandist, and he regarded these roles as inseparable. His province, he said, was "to rouse with words and animate with the voice." To him "the Druids were the chaplains of our ancestors among the Germans. These by their words incited to war, and inspired the valor of the combatants. The bards were the chaplains of the aborigines of Britain. O! Ossian bard of Fingal!"

Caught up in the Revolutionary activity that promised the fulfillment of "Rising Glory," Brackenridge subdued the ideal of moderation that had been implanted by his classical studies:

Let the streets of Boston and the bloody fifth of March [the Boston Massacre, 1770] be witness of his [King George's] cruelty, when several lovely and unresisting youths fell by the hands of the bloody Preston [sergeant of the guard] who acted the savage pleasure of his still more savage master. Let the streets that were wet with this blood and drank it not, for the flood ran down the stones, let the streets that were wet and ran down with this blood speak loud of it and cry to heaven for a day of vengeance. Let the town of Boston be witness to their cruelty. The town of Boston with the cries of infants, and the groans of distressed mothers detained from their relatives and husbands. . . . Let the heights of Boston [Bunker Hill], naked of the sister town which stood upon them, be witness to the tyranny and, at the same time, some part of the punishment of Britain; for the heroes saw themselves revenged and slept not in death until fifteen hundred of the foe lay vanquished on the soil.[12]

The lack of theological sentiment in his sermons must have revealed to him that he was not a man of God but of men. His son stated that his "natural temperament called him to scenes of active life." He merely respected religion, according to his son, because it was "necessary to the well being of society." What he reverenced in Christianity was its literature. Along with the classics, the scriptures taught universal lessons of behavior necessary for success in the democratic experiment.

In "Biographical Notice," Henry Marie Brackenridge renders a more positive interpretation of his father's religious attitude: "His writings display a liberality on the subject of religion, which is thought by some to border on free thinking. It is true he hated hypocrisy but reverenced the Christian religion as taught in the scriptures: he was only skeptical as to some tenets of the different sects." However, in *Recollections of Persons and Places in the West* (1834), Henry Marie reveals his father's almost total neglect of Christian indoctrination for his son: "My religious and moral principles were left to spring up spontaneously, the cultivation of the intellect being erroneously considered all

sufficient. . . . Vice and impiety may be regarded as follies in the
eye of reason, and the mind rightly trained may be supposed
to view them in that light; and such was the philosophy of my
father who was a perfectly honest man."

IV *Philadelphia Man of Letters*

Shortly after the British evacuated Philadelphia in 1778,
Brackenridge abandoned the rather hypocritical role of chaplain
in the army and went to the city to seek a career in literature.
Although no American magazine had yet succeeded, Brackenridge had boldly conceived of a periodical that would ingrain
the values of literature in the new American civilization. Casting
aside second thoughts that "the public will not sufficiently attend to the expense of the press," he ploughed about a thousand pounds into the venture. According to his son, the invest-
ment "depreciated so rapidly that in a short time he was stripped
of the labor of years."

The chaos of the newly freed city contributed largely to the
failure of the magazine. The Tories were trying to secure life and
property against the threats of revengeful, triumphant Whigs.
And Whigs, no longer bound against a common enemy, fractured
violently—conservative versus radical. Prices were soaring, credit
was wanting, and paper money flowed as from a stream. Boldly,
the sharpers came out of their corners. The belles spun webs of
gaiety and raucous festivity, perhaps to cover recent misadven-
tures among the retreated. In the midst of reckless extravagance,
the mobs demonstrated their violent tempers. Had Brackenridge
taken account of this social breakdown, he might have increased
his chances for success; but he assumed that the literary interests
of his audience were his own. Still in the grand manner, he appealed for support to the multifarious tastes of statesmen,
soldiers, farmers, tradesmen, virgin maids, widows, and wives:

> Statesmen of assembly great;
> Soldiers that on danger wait;
> Farmers that subdue the plain;
> Merchants that attempt the main;
> Tradesmen who their labours ply;
> These shall court thy company:
> These shall say with placid vein,
> Have you read the Magazine?

Maids of Virgin-beauty fair;
Widows gay and debonnair;
Matrons of a graver age;
Wives whom household cares engage;
These shall hear of thee and learn,
To esteem thee more than Sterne.
These shall say when thou art seen,
Oh! enchanting magazine.[13]

Although the magazine endured an entire year, Brackenridge probably foresaw its doom after the fifth or sixth issue and turned to the study of law in order to prepare himself for a livelihood. Several early issues contained a serialized history, "Establishment of the United States," which was never completed because its busy author became engaged in "other arduous studies."[14]

On July 5, 1779, about the time he discontinued writing the "Establishment of the United States," Brackenridge delivered an address to an august assembly that included the President of the United States, members of Congress, and the Minister of France. The address, *An Eulogium of the Brave Men who have Fallen in the Contest with Great Britain,* revitalized his taste for oratory and perhaps recalled to the center of his mind the impression of Attorney Samuel Chase in action.

As editor of the *United States Magazine* and as the author of the *Political Discourses,* he enjoyed the reputation of a Philadelphia man of letters; but even a successful writer and editor could not receive the immediate response to his work the way Samuel Chase could. Asked to deliver the principal address at the elaborate ceremonies planned by the Constitutional Society of Philadelphia to celebrate the anniversary of Independence, he was not unaware of new opportunity. Amid much pomp—odes were sung at proper pauses in his delivery—Brackenridge described, in the august tones of his commencement glories, the patriotic sacrifices made by every citizen, as well as those made by the brave men who had fallen in the war with a tyrannical and brutish enemy. The fervid prose rhythms conveyed rather shocking views of British atrocities, but the rhetorical skill prevented a clash between the realistic content and the grand style of its transmission.

His oratorical triumph opened a new vista and thus softened his imminent journalistic defeat. Because he was an orderly man he waited to discontinue publication until December, when the *United States Magazine* had run a full year. Then he blamed both the inflated finances of the new nation and the audience:

> . . . persons who are disaffected to the cause of America. These have been sorely pricked and buffeted with the sharp points of Whiggism, which, like arrows from the great machines of Archimedes, have been darted out from it [the magazine]. They have been sorely injured by these points and will be ready to believe that in the suspension of this work is accomplished that prophecy of the Apocalypse, "And Satan shall be bound a thousand years." There is yet another class of men that will be sensible of some happiness now that the mouth of this publication is in a fair way to be at length closed; I mean the people who inhabit the region of stupidity and cannot bear to have the tranquility of their repose disturbed by the villainous jargon of a book.[15]

Brackenridge temporarily gave up his literary career; he left for Annapolis to seek Samuel Chase and formal training in the law.

CHAPTER 3

Frontier Realities

AN ALLEGORY can be traced in the serialized story, "Cave of Vanhest," which ran from January through July, 1779, in the *United States Magazine*. The story ends with the narrator's turning from his present love, Miss Law, to the ladies of the cave, who represent beauty in nature. This story may symbolize the conflicting desires that Brackenridge carried West in the spring of 1781. Attraction to the ladies in the cave recalls his earlier desire for "some sequestered vale . . . far from converse and the social band . . . on some Western hill," which he described in "Poem on The Divine Revelation." And the love of Miss Law, he explained years later, was only a means to an end: "When I left Philadelphia almost twenty years ago, I saw no chance of being anything in that city, there were such great men before me. . . . I pushed my way to these woods where I thought I might emerge one day, and get forward myself in a congress or some other public body."[1] Getting forward did not mean to Brackenridge the abandoning of his democratic and cultural concepts. These, too, were carried across the Alleghenies to the wild Ohio country.

In 1781 the road out of Philadelphia, America's center of culture and politics, narrowed to a horse trail across the mountains and led to the small village of Pittsburgh at the junction of the Allegheny and Monongahela rivers. Brackenridge found the village "not distinguished by house or street." The hub consisted of mean log houses that had grown squalid through years of brisk trading in flour and skins; now pioneer families bound for Kentucky floated on down the Ohio River without stopping for supplies as they used to do. Nevertheless, "it appeared to me as what would one day be a town of note; and in the meantime might be pushed forward by the usual means which raise such places."[2] He had no difficulty implanting himself among the Scotch-Irish inhabitants, many of them from the Barrens of his boyhood. But Brackenridge was not inclined to adapt himself to their crudities and bumptiousness after so many years of sophisticated society; instead, he decided to adapt the place to his personality. He meant to civilize it, to root all his cultural goods in this crude incubator of the nation: "I had a strong interest to prompt me to offer myself to that place. My object was to advance the country and thereby myself."[3]

I *Seeding from the East*

After admission to the rural bar in April, 1781, he became engulfed almost immediately in the popular separatist movement sparked by former Virginians who resented the boundary change that had made Pennsylvanians of them. The separatist movement was fortified by a majority of frontiersmen who felt that the national government had not supported them in their constant struggles with the Indians. His loyalty to the Federal government yet untarnished, Brackenridge acted according to his ideals and thus against the popular will, a mode of behavior that was to become characteristic. He convinced members of the State Assembly to pass a law declaring any agitation for setting up a new state to be a treasonable act. To oppose the demands of the frontiersmen on the frontier was to oppose oneself. The principle of the national good as more important than the local or personal good was an entrapping subtlety out of the East. Twenty years later, Brackenridge reflected: "If I had known the little account to which this turned afterwards by the mismanagement of the legislature and the land office and speculators . . . and all these things obstructing the improvement and population of the country, I might have thought less of the value of my efforts on this occasion."[4]

His first literary efforts on the frontier indicated that he had given up the muse: they were shocking exposés of Indian atrocities. The occasion for these narratives was a punitive expedition under Colonel Crawford against the Indians on the Sandusky River in the summer of 1782. It ended in the rout of the white men and the capture, torture, and death of Colonel

Crawford and many of his troops. The sensationalism of these reports testifies to the author's own shock which he tried to transmit. The preface reveals that he had been "so long unaccustomed to write, I scarcely have resolution to put pen to paper." It is apparent that during the two years before Brackenridge renewed his writing, the reality of the frontier had at least jarred the literary attitudes of his years in the East.

The next year, however, he produced a masque in the courtly style of Ben Jonson, perhaps to convince himself that he was still a literary man. But its naiads, jocund dieties, and spirits of the springs and rivers refused to dance on the frontier as they had in England more than a century before. The masque was written and then performed at Warm Springs, Virginia in 1784 to honor General Washington, who was also visiting there:

> You are still, pure streams, the same.
> Emblem this of that great chief,
> WASHINGTON who made us free,
> Shewing midst our joy and grief
> Equal equanimity.[5]

Washington's diary for that day records hours spent in arranging for the construction of buildings on his property in that town but does not mention Brackenridge or his masque. Perhaps the cool reception of these honors inspired Brackenridge to oppose the general in court the following year when he defended thirteen settlers who were squatting on land Washington had purchased from a Colonel Groghan. Arguing that Groghan had bought the land from the Indians—and therefore that it was not his land to sell since land could not really be purchased from Indians who didn't own it—he lost. The squatters were ejected. In poetry, Brackenridge did not revert again to the grand manner until 1801 when his zeal for Jefferson inspired him to write an eulogy, "In Imitation of Virgil's Pollio."

By 1785 Brackenridge occupied a leading position at the bar, had married, and had become a man of property.[6] A narrative he produced that year reveals a mature development of the storyteller's art as well as a ripened sense of realism. Another Indian narrative, it was written because "I was curious." He wished to understand the Indian mind and motive. A carpenter working on his house had been killed by an Indian, Mamachtaga, on a drunken spree. In spite of Brackenridge's loathing for the "savages vulgarly called Indians," he offered to defend the accused. His decision aroused the frontiersmen who threatened to storm the prison and to hang the Indian awaiting trial.

If frontier reality had invaded his literary attitudes and his style, it had not yet affected his political ideas. Mamachtaga's trial had increased the frontiersmen's distrust of the independent, unpredictable literary lawyer. No man defending Indians could be accepted by the settlers. If he were to influence the cultural development of the frontier people, Brackenridge realized he would need a forum in which he could appeal to their logic. He believed that he could convince them through reason. He could demonstrate, for example, that education was their most pressing need; and, to carry out actions in their interests, he would represent them in the State Assembly. Consequently, he sought means of founding a frontier newspaper which would serve both as a forum and as an instrument for his election to the Pennsylvania legislature. The idea of a frontier newspaper had been in his mind since the day he left Philadelphia: "I had an ambition; or rather I obeyed the impulse of my mind in being among the first to bring the press to the west of the mountains."[7]

He induced two young Philadelphians, John Scull and Joseph Hall, to bring a press across the mountains and "try the unpromising venture." The first issue of the *Pittsburgh Gazette* was pulled from the press on July 29, 1785. Brackenridge's contribution was an idealized "Account of Pittsburgh," in which he "intended to give some reputation to the town with a view to induce emigration to this particular spot." This idyllic description of Pittsburgh exaggerated the numbers of dwellings and residents along with "the breezes of the river, coming from the Mississippi and the ocean; the gales that fan the woods . . . the prospect of extensive hills and dales whence the fragrant air brings odours of a thousand flowers. . . . How pleasant by a crystal fountain in a tea party under one of those hills with the rivers and the plains beneath. . . ." He could perceive no more "delightful spot under heaven to spend the summer months." Ignoring the filth-strewn streets, the crude log constructions, and the ignorance of the inhabitants, the author saw glorious works arising in this wonder city of the West.

Although Brackenridge used the newspaper for his own

political progress, he identified this progress with the cultural advancement of the people—not a particularly popular cause. Through the columns of the *Pittsburgh Gazette* he tried to instill desires for learning, for literary arts, and for civic establishments —an academy, a church, a bookstore, and a lending library. In his appeals, he expanded the spirit of "Rising Glory" to all the population. The appeals were expressed in direct prose and empowered with the fiery metaphors found in his sermons to the troops:

> . . . a few eminent men in any period, have usually given the tone, so to speak, to a whole nation, nay sometimes to a whole age. They have been the authors of that superiority which an age has obtained over another. To give examples from our own country; a few men at the beginning of this revolution, discovered the limits of the authority of Britain, and pointed out our just rights. The cultivated genius of these men, through the darkness of a night which might otherwise have involved the continent, flashed fires, and gave the flame of Aetnas. What then must be the strength and dignity of a government where eminent genius is everywhere called forth by education. Academies are the furnaces which melt the natural ore to real metal. . . . Cultivated genius has the power of electric fire.[8]

II *The People's Unpopular Representative*

On September 9, 1786, one week after his last article promoting civic development appeared in the *Pittsburgh Gazette*, Brackenridge announced his candidacy for the State Assembly. If not elected, he concluded, "there is no harm done." Then, realizing the limited appeal of his educated manner, Brackenridge shrewdly wooed support in the guise of frontier characters. Adopting pseudonyms, he wrote letters to the *Gazette*, repeating his own utterances and attacking the actions of Congress and of the Western representatives to the State Assembly. More significant than the criticisms are the images in which he rendered them. The "Letter from Angus MacMore," for example, contains invaluable local-color glimpses of real life and its conditions on the frontier:

> I have been a subscriber from the list, and sent in a dollar the other day by William Guy when he went to the contractor's store to buy an ounce of snuff for his wife. Our neighbors think a great

deal of the paper, and I have as many of them about me between sermons on a Sunday to hear the news, as Mathew M'Connel has on his justice days when come about the law business. I see the Congress have appointed a superintendant of the Indians to give them presents to keep them in peace. I am persuaded it is meant well and the men may be capable that are nominated to this station, but I am apprehensive. . . .

His campaign articles promised to work for the people's interests; but these interests, he specifically told them, were primarily cultural: "I conceive it to be a public good to this country that the town of Pittsburgh be encouraged, that it be made a borough, that it have a seat of justice, that it have a school endowed in it." Secondarily, he appealed to local self-interest—the American rights to navigation on the Mississippi then held by Spain— an interest which he shared. However, his legal mind caused him to equivocate about the settlers' most urgent desire—titles to their land and payment for it with state certificates of indebtedness. The settlers believed Brackenridge was saying that he would promote a bill permitting them to do so. Actually he told them "We entertain the hope that even this session a law will be enacted" allowing payment by certificate. And, though "it ought to be strongly urged," he did not commit himself to the urging.[9]

Elected, perhaps because of his implications rather than his assertions, Brackenridge opposed the bill when debate opened. He had been convinced that "it would be injurious to the interests of the people in the Western country." He informed the electorate of this decision in a letter to the *Gazette,* which he now employed as a channel of news and interpretation of legislative activity. His concept of a representative included the function of reporting to his electors what he did and why. He saw that the democratic experiment could not succeed without a basis for intelligent public decision, and his reports provided this basis for his constituents. On this occasion, Brackenridge explained: "It was extremely difficult for people in his part of the country to obtain enough money to pay for certificates, to warrant the land they had a right to by occupancy, and as this measure would tend to raise them still higher, and so make it more difficult, [I] was opposed to it."

The backwoods reaction to this political and economic lesson was volatile. He had violated his word and turned against his people. He was in sympathy with the Eastern aristocrats; he was a traitor. A letter printed in the *Pittsburgh Gazette* claimed that he had "sold the good will of his country for a dinner of some stockholder's fat beef."[10] In Philadelphia, Brackenridge did not yet know that his report, which indicated his trust in the reasoning powers of his electors, had spelled his doom. He continued sending reports of the accomplishments he had promised, of the academy bill he had introduced, of a petition to improve the roads, and of a bill to incorporate "a religious Christian Society in Pittsburgh."

When the assembly recessed, he came home to face a storm. The backwoodsmen had shifted their aspirations to the shoulders of William Findley, their other representative in the State Assembly. Assuming the role of the people's champion, Findley drew an image of Brackenridge as their enemy: "a gentleman who professes the greatest acquired abilities, and most shining imagination, [but who] makes a prey of the people's confidence, betrays their interests and trifles with his own solemn professions, he may expect the people to look upon him with indignation and treat him with contempt." Most painful perhaps was Findley's reference to his practice of reporting the reasons for his legislative actions: "by putting a few lines in the newspaper, he would reconcile them to his views; this, however, I would have passed over as an explosion of unguarded vanity, had I not seen his delusory attempt to impose upon the people by his insidious observations of this business in your newspaper."[11]

Findley's observations were also printed in the *Pittsburgh Gazette*. The irony had a second twist, a deeper thrust unknown to Findley. When James Hall died on November 10, Scull sent a letter offering Brackenridge half ownership of the *Gazette*. The political advantages must have caused at least a moment's hesitation, but Brackenridge decided not to compromise his concept of the press as a forum necessary to the success of the democratic experiment. He arranged for the purchase of Hall's share by John Boyd, a Philadelphian who "now sets out to settle in our town."[12]

His home life was disintegrating along with his political career. Mrs. Brackenridge died that winter and arrangements were made

to board Henry Marie with a cobbler's family who rented a log
cabin on the Brackenridge property. Yet Brackenridge showed
little disillusionment or defeat. He fought back, answering Findley in a series of articles addressed "To the Inhabitants of the
Western Country." One of these stated his concept of a representative:

> If the representative had not a latitude of reflection notwithstand-
> ing every former sentiment, how could he act consistent with his
> oath when he takes his seat in the house. . . . From this oath it
> must appear that a representative is not supposed to be a mere
> machine, like a clock wound up, to run for many hours in the
> same way; he is sent to hear from others, and to think for himself,
> as well as to vote. . . . I proposed a number of points to the
> people, and this case of certificates is the only one, with respect
> to which I changed my mind: I have laboured diligently to ac-
> complish all the rest. . . . It is certain the people do not always
> know their own interest, nor do individuals know.

Abstract philosophizing about representative government, however, was no more effective than appeals to reason. It was no
substitute for the fulfillment of desires, and it sounded rather
insulting. The more he explained, the more he condemned himself. Returning for the second session of the Assembly, he
realized that his approaches to the people were useless. As he
recorded later:

> There were two parties at the time in the house known under
> the name of constitutional and anti-constitutional. The Western
> members were constitutionalists, I was therefore obliged to join
> the anti-constitutionalists. . . . I was represented as a traitor
> who had betrayed my country. . . . They were 9 to 1 against me:
> Findley was at the head of them, and I had thought to have
> defended myself by writing, but only made the matter worse, for
> the people thought it impossible that plain simple men could be
> wrong, and a profane lawyer right.[13]

As an anti-constitutionalist, he managed to attain the land
endowment for the Pittsburgh Academy and to get a bill
through the Assembly providing for the new county of Allegheny
with a court seat at Pittsburgh. He sponsored another bill establishing a non-sectarian church for the town. After a Pittsburgh
minister had manipulated a change from a non-sectarian to a

Presbyterian congregation, the people's rather wayward representative reported to them on March 17, 1787:

> I had hoped that seated on the utmost verge of the inhabited globe, and separated from the Old World by a great mountain, you would have taken up things on the first principles, and represented a church like those in the time of the first apostles, distinguished by the name of *Christian* only, and have left it to divines in future times to dispute, as they now do, about those of Smyrna or Ephesus, whether you are Presbyterian or Episcopal.

When the bill was passed, it established a Presbyterian church in Pittsburgh; passionately Brackenridge told the Assembly, "The people of that town were all well disposed to remain under one roof; but whenever priests come they make trouble." In the *Gazette* he continued to promote his community church concept, revealing his role in bringing the first minister to the town and in arousing public desire for a house of worship. Again he described the kind of church needed to fulfill the community functions: it was not to be associated with a synod; but the minister might attend the synod if he wished, and if his absence would not detract from his duties. Any person of ecclesiastical character would be permitted to preach. The form of worship would be of no consequence. Presbyterianism would do if not called by that name. Only the name "Christian" would be suitable for a church of Christians. The roots of the concept are democratic and economic. The town did not have enough people to support more than one church, but a Presbyterian church would be discriminatory because it would ignore the other denominations.

Alliance with the anti-constitutionalists had allowed Brackenridge to obtain legislation benefiting the Westerners; the constitutionalists, whom the frontiersmen favored, could not have passed these bills since they were in the minority. The significance of these benefits, however, faded in the light of the new Federal Constitution that now came before the Assembly for debate. Fearing that a strong central government would impose higher taxes and limit liberties, the Western constitutionalists opposed it. The anti-constitutionalists, who could not abide the loose government provided by the existing constitution, favored the new, stronger document. Now Brackenridge joined the

Easterners in spirit as well as fact—and lost whatever popularity his bills favoring the West might have regained for him. Indeed, he summoned all his literary powers to secure acceptance of the new Constitution.

Since direct reasoning had failed to convince, he tried now to move the populace through irony, resorting to his early mode of satire, and through eloquence, resorting to sermons. In the *Gazette* earlier that year (March 24, 1787), while he still hoped to revive his political fortune, Brackenridge had partially conceded to Findley's accusations that he had called the backwoodsmen "fools" and "prowling wolves." Any malignant person, he told the frontiersmen, could deliberately conceal the intention of his words by cleverly removing them from context: "I am not the most guarded person in my speech." But whatever caution he may have instituted in his speech was now abandoned in the struggle to gain support for the new Constitution. Reminiscing twenty years later, he wrote, "Ridicule is not the test of truth, but it may be employed to expose error, and on this occasion it seemed not amiss to use it a little, as a great object was at stake, and much wilful misrepresentation to be encountered . . . [it] contributed a little to consolidate the government of the union which, after all the pains taken, was with great difficulty brought about."[14]

III *The Birth of Teague O'Regan*

In October, 1787, the Assembly voted to call a convention to ratify or refuse the new Federal Constitution. Nineteen Western members, led by William Findley, voted against the measure; they took leave immediately then seeing their imminent defeat in order to avoid a quorum. The sergeant-at-arms and an assistant clerk pursued them through the streets of Philadelphia and managed to corner two of them. Forcibly returned to their places in the Assembly, these representatives tried devious means of escape but were successfully restrained until the vital business of establishing the time, place, and procedure of the convention was transacted.

Brackenridge, the only Western representative to favor the new Constitution, lashed out against the anti-Federalists with a series of Hudibrastic satires in which Findley, who had been a clothmaker, became Traddle, the ambitious but ignorant weaver who should have stayed home at his treadle. Later when Findley, rather than Brackenridge, was elected to the ratifying convention, the infuriated satirist substituted the lowest common denominator of the time for his Assembly colleague, Teague O'Regan, the people's choice. Thus, the theme and the leading character for *Modern Chivalry* evolved out of the author's embroilments, disappointments, stained ideals, and the realities of the whirling events that generated national attitudes.

If fervor for the new Constitution had inadvertently fertilized literary seeds in Brackenridge, it had also destroyed his political career and wrecked his law practice. Convinced by Findley that the new Constitution was a devilish instrument aimed at raising taxes and replacing freedom with shackles, the backwoodsmen callously ignored Brackenridge. They shunned his law office and his appeals for re-election to the Assembly. After he returned to Pittsburgh as a private citizen in the autumn of 1787, he continued his effort to overcome Western prejudice against the new instrument of government. He satirized the opposition in a series of letters to the *Gazette*. In one of them (May 10, 1788) he assumes the role of a constituent who ironically reduces the actions of William Findley to the absurd: "I acknowledge this will considerably affect the system of education, alertness and speed of foot becoming the necessary qualification of a legislator, for if a member is not swift in running off, the check may be lost, the vote being taken before he fairly disappears. There will hence be two kinds of motion in the House, that to the speaker and the other to the door." In "Cursory Remarks on the Federal Constitution" (March 1), his caricature stood on less substantial ground. Among the objections to the new Constitution was a lack of a Bill of Rights. "What is the nature of a bill of rights?" he asked. "It is a schedule of inventory of those powers which the Congress do not possess. But if it clearly ascertained what powers they have, what need of a catalogue of those powers which they have not?"

Sensing little progress with the Westerners, he turned finally to sermons: "O Israel," he lamented to the lambs who would not follow his word, "thou art destroyed for lack of knowledge," and "Oh my people, they which lead thee cause thee to err, and destroy the way of thy path." His pride reduced through personal and political loss, he pleaded with the wayward to follow the righteous path of democracy, a "religion" for which Brackenridge had become a prophet.

Having nothing to gain personally, Brackenridge spoke out of altruism. The "Sermons in Favor of the Federal Constitution" are similar in tone and intent to the fiery *Political Discourses* of his Revolutionary days. The evils of American demagoguery had replaced those of British tyranny. If the people are informed and are led by men who place the national good above their selfish ambitions, they could not possibly oppose the new Constitution. The sermons defeated themselves, however, by offering evidence that all through history the people had been uninformed and had rejected the leadership of the educated and dedicated for that of the demagogues:

It would be well if they [opposers of the new Constitution] were capable of leading in the right course. But this is not the case; they cause the people of this country to err by their vain babblings. The consequence is not only disgrace but injury. While we become the object of ridicule abroad, we obstruct our happiness at home. What man who had great household affairs to adjust, extensive mercantile or even farming concerns to manage would entrust them with those persons? Yet you entrust the management of the Commonwealth to them, and when they act contrary to the wisdom of men of real understanding in these affairs you permit your senses to be deceived by the vile nonsense which they utter to excuse their conduct. By these means the "way of your paths" or your path way is disturbed; that is, you are impeded or altogether thrown out of the proper course in your progress to wealth and happiness.

But is this any prodigy or wonderful thing? Far from it. It has always been and will always be the case in some degree while human nature remains the same. On this head examples are brought every day from the Greek and Roman history. But that of the Jews is sufficiently fraught with such. Isaiah, the author of the words prefixed to this discourse, was a man of a noble mind, educated in the schools of the prophets, and possessing great understanding. It would naturally be imagined that such a man would be heard with attention and that his advice would be received. Not so. It appears that there were persons who had the ear of the populace, demagogues, who could do with them as they pleased.

It is his language, "Oh, my people, they which lead thee cause thee to err, and destroy the way of thy paths."[15]

When the controversy ended with adoption of the Constitution in June, 1788, most of the residents who had opposed it gathered to celebrate. According to the *Pittsburgh Gazette,* some fifteen hundred inhabitants of the Western country "occupying the verge of [a] hill . . . were addressed by Mr. Brackenridge as follows: 'Oh my compatriots, I have great news to give you. . . .'" As he finished, the crowd cheered and tossed hats in the air. Then the people lit bonfires to each state of the Union.

Taking the ovation as a belated recognition of his policies, Brackenridge sought to oppose Findley, the anti-Federalist candidate to the First Congress of the newly formed government. The Federalists, however, refused to place Brackenridge's name on the ticket; apparently, they could not consider this individualist, who had first joined them by default, among the party regulars. They suspected him of sympathy with the backwoods objectors to the Federal excises. They remembered how the frontiersmen had amused themselves at the expense of the exciseman, William Graham, "singeing his wig, cutting the tail of his horse, putting coals in his boots," and later "besieg[ing] him in a public house,"[16] nearly killing him. Brackenridge had defended these rioters when they were brought to trial in 1785. "It is to be presumed," he admitted later, "that I had been of the same opinion with my clients, that excise laws were odious." Distrusted by all, Brackenridge declared himself "absolved from all engagements to the party." Though he had gained his object—acceptance of the new Federal government in the West—the personal suffering it caused him endured: "My character was totally gone with the populace. My practice lost. . . . Pride and good policy would not permit me to leave the country, until I had conquered the prejudice. . . . It was the first experience I had ever had in my life of unpopularity, and I found it a thing . . . painful to sustain and . . . difficult to remove. . . ."[17]

Now a private citizen, his tenacity to ideals no longer menaced the frontiersmen. They merely thought him to be somewhat eccentric; but, according to his son, "he always denied the charge and asserted that he was the only one of his acquaintances that was like everybody else. . . . [His time was] chiefly passed at his office in the village, being entirely devoted to books and business." Though rebuilding his law practice was a necessity, his "love of letters [his son observed] was such that he always begrudged the time devoted to the drudgery of business; and nothing so effectually tried his patience as the idle delay of a client after his business was accomplished. . . . [And he] made it a point to discourage litigation . . . 'Go away, sir; no man of sense goes to law,'" he would say, "'Did you ever hear of my going to law?'"[18] On two occasions, at least, Brackenridge settled his disputes with force: once when an assailant clubbed him on the shoulder without warning, and again when an over-wrought citizen named Simpson drew a sword in the back room of an inn. Simpson was dropped first by a hurled chair, his weapon was smashed, and finally he was singed when Bracken-ridge tossed him onto the glowing hearth.

A powerfully built man with a high, polished forehead, a large nose and florid face, Brackenridge presented a most fearsome countenance to Henry Marie, who tells of his fear of the switch in the hand of his father. Discovering an "improvable intellect" in his two-year-old son, Brackenridge obtained a hornbook and with "considerable cruelty" forced the child to "the hard task of constant application." Aside from the task of disciplining the boy's mind, Brackenridge took little notice of his son.

Nor did he attend much to the business of the town, a tight community where, it appeared to him, inhabitants were "stowed away like persons in a jail, or on board a man of war."[19] During the year 1789, however, he broke his silence to chastise the villagers on matters of conduct. He wrote a sermon on village gossip because no clergyman had undertaken the task of im-proving the town's morals. And he wrote another on dueling, introduced by the following letters in Scull's *Pittsburgh Gazette* of June 13:

Mr. Scull,

The age of chivalry is not over, and challenges . . . have been given even in the midst of a yellow fever, which one would think was killing people fast enough already. The fear of God or the law are usual and just grounds of refusing; but I will give you a sample of the way in which I got off with some of my challenges, in the following letter and answer on a late occasion, but omitting the name of the challenger, as I have no inclination to trouble him with a prosecution.

Sir,

I will thank you to take a walk with a friend and meet me at the back of the graveyard about sunrise tomorrow morning. After what has happened, you know what I mean.

Your humble servant, etc.

Sir,

I know what you mean very well; you want to have a shot at me, but I have no inclination to hit you, and I am afraid you would hit me. I pray thee therefore have me excused.

The sermon that followed was based on 2 Sam. iii, 13: "And the king lamented over Abner, and said 'Died Abner as a fool dieth.' " From the letter to Scull, it is apparent that some satiric view of contemporary chivalry—later to appear in *Modern Chivalry*—was incubating during Brackenridge's public quiescence.

In 1790, John Pope, a visitor to Pittsburgh who found "scoundrels infesting the place," was somewhat perplexed that this town should be the home of "the celebrated Hugh Henry Brackenridge, author of the six political sermons . . . and of various other tracts since."[20] Upon acquaintance with the "celebrated" Brackenridge, however, the traveler drew an impression akin to that of the townsmen; he was indeed an unusual man. The circumstances of the lawyer's second marriage particularly intrigued Pope:

Mr. Brackenridge on his way from Washington Court, called in at Mr. Wolfe's to have his horse fed and escape a rain which was then descending. The horse was fed, the rain had subsided, and Mr. Brackenridge to avoid wet feet ordered his horse to be brought to the door. Miss Wolfe was directed to perform that office.

> Nut brown were her Locks, her Shape was
> full straight
> Her eyes were as black as a Sloe
> Milk white were her Teeth, full smart
> was her Gait
> And sleek was her Skin as a Doe.

. . . He had not gone more than a Sabbath day's journey before his horse at the instigation of the rider, turned short about and revisited Mr. Wolfe's. A familiar application was made to the old gentleman for his daughter which he considered as nothing more than pleasantry in Mr. Brackenridge for which he is remarkable. Mr. Brackenridge declared that he was serious, that his intentions were honourable, and that his future Happiness rested on the event of his then application. Miss Sabina had been employed in shrubbing the old man's meadow which saved him the annual expense of about ten dollars. This with him was an unsuperable objection to parting with this girl—Mr. Brackenridge obviated the difficulty by paying down a sum of money, obtaining the young lady's consent, married her and sent her to Philadelphia where she is now under the governance of a reputable female character whose business will be to polish the manners and wipe off the rusticities which Mrs. Brackenridge had acquired whilst a Wolfe.[21]

The marriage was undertaken with the brusqueness of other business matters, perhaps for similar reasons. By 1790 Brackenridge had arrived at the literary form in which he would cast his satirical portrait of democratic folly; and, at the time of his marriage, he was at work on *Modern Chivalry*.

IV *"Citizen Brackenridge" and the Whiskey Rebels*

Although Brackenridge had resigned from public life when he started *Modern Chivalry*, he had been drawn back into it before he had completed the first volume. He began to attack the Federalists who had rejected him, and he was particularly critical of Hamilton's taxation system which imposed levies on whiskey, the chief product of the frontier. He was also critical of the government's pro-British attitude. Effectively, it was anti-French, but Washington labeled it "neutralism." In Western minds the excise tax and the government's British leanings were aspects of a conspiracy against the frontiersmen. Westerners had formed small democratic societies in imitation of the French Jacobins. These promoted the cause of American aid to the new French Republic in her struggle with England, and this cause symbolized for Westerners the democratic defiance of European monarchy. Their interests were represented in government by Thomas Jefferson, the Secretary of State.

For Brackenridge, frontier interests had become identical with those of the nation. In spite of the violent excesses of the French, their struggle with monarchy was another part of the democratic struggle with aristocracy, as represented in America by the conflict between Jefferson and Hamilton. In the West, the excise tax symbolized aristocratic dominion, as pre-Revolutionary taxes had symbolized British dominion. It represented all the Western resentment of the Federalist policies of Washington and Hamilton. The settlers also resented the Spanish rights to navigation of the Mississippi, the government's apparent disinterest in protecting them from Indians, and its failure to settle Western land disputes equitably.

Almost from Brackenridge's first days in the West, he had opposed the whiskey tax; but he did not join any organization actively resisting it. Findley, the demagogue, was the Western champion; and Brackenridge said that he "did not like to be ostensibly in the same party."[22] Although he denounced the excise tax, he also denounced forceful opposition to the government. Clinging to ideas that forced him out of both parties, he was caught between conflicting demands of his conscience—sympathy with the cause of the insurgents and loyalty to his government—when the parties clashed in the Whiskey Rebellion in Pennsylvania in 1794. The internal conflict led him into the role of mediator which earned him the distrust and scorn of both sides and exposed him to charges of treason.

That he had been a traitor to the Federal government and that he had been an instigator of the insurrection were apparent to Secretary Hamilton. In 1792, while in Philadelphia arranging to publish the first two volumes of *Modern Chivalry*, Brackenridge had written a series of inflammatory essays for the *National Gazette*, edited by "that rascal, Freneau." One had struck at Washington's foreign policy by accusing the British of arming and provoking the Indians to attack frontier settlements. Another directly attacked the excise laws claiming that the government was a coalition of money interests and aristocrats in the richer capitals, and was "opposed to the bed of simplicity and true republicanism." He rendered an image of this bed of simplicity and republicanism by describing the frontier sources of discontent, the conditions in which the frontiersman lived, and the extra hardships inflicted through the excise on whiskey. The essay requested relief from the burden of the excise, and in return promised the Federal government great profits from the Western country.

The tone is similar to that of the sermons on the Federal Constitution. Pleading humbly, Brackenridge refers frequently to his lack of power and to his reduced position. Yet in spite of this tone, his warning that the oppression imposed by the excise could not be borne indefinitely, that the frontiersmen would eventually "resist with intemperance what they ought to resist with reason," was later taken by Federalists as a threat of insurrection:

> . . . let them have a little time to breath and recover loss and feel vigour, and if they do not submit to every demand of contribution to the revenue, I shall be the first to bear testimony against them in their country, as I have done heretofore when I thought them wrong. But I know the yeomanry are honest, though sometimes misled, and in due time that country will afford both by trade and tax a substantial revenue to these states, but oppression will make the wise mad, and induce them to resist with intemperance what they ought to resist with reason.

With this essay Brackenridge resumed his role as pastor of the people and became a prophet of their future. Indeed, he anticipated the antagonism that led to the Civil War, predicting the role of the West as a balance between the East and the South. Unless that balance was restored, he could see only destruction of all that had been accomplished through "our wars and victories." The balance could be restored only by allowing the West to share the governmental benefits enjoyed in the other parts of the country: "I consider the Western country as the *tiers etat,* or third estate of the Union, and, as necessary to hold the balance in the interests of the East and South parts. There is nothing, in my contemplation [that] will contribute more to the duration of our empire than such balance."[23]

At home, however, he refused to serve on the committees which were organized to protest and even to act against the whiskey tax law—or for the cause of the French Revolutionists which most Westerners watched as a test of the success of democracy. He was, after all, a man of law. Sidestepping active entanglements with the budding insurrectionists, Brackenridge nevertheless abetted them with his fiery orations and ironic satires. Flippantly, he celebrated the execution of Louis XVI by sending a bite-sized satire to Freneau's *National Gazette* (April 20, 1798) entitled "Louis Capet Lost his Caput."

During his Independence Day oration five years earlier, Brackenridge had praised Louis for his aid to America in the Revolution; but now a republic had been born at the monarch's expense and republicanism was a higher principle than gratitude. Why then, Brackenridge asked, "such a noise even with republicans about the death of Louis?" Had his brother kings and aristocrats received the news of the "trucidation of democrats . . . they would have snuffed the air that brought the account, as if fragrant with odoriferous odors." The principle was significant, not the execution of the man Louis. To Brackenridge it appeared that the Federalists of the East governed without principle; they had opposed monarchy but were now shocked by its fall.

When Washington issued his proclamation on neutrality in response to the French declaration of war on the British, Brackenridge published in the *Gazette* of May 15 a letter "To the President" in which he asserted his principle that neutrality is impossible. All men are involved in any war between oppressor and oppressed. Thus, "the cause of France is the cause of man," and "neutrality is desertion." The letter strongly asserts Western suspicion that neutrality is a guise used by the Federalists to seek favor with the despots of Europe.

On July 4, 1793, Brackenridge soared to the apogee of his French fervor. Addressing a patriotic celebration in Pittsburgh, his oratory flamed as it had before in the battle camps of the American Revolution:

> Shall kings combine, and shall republics not unite? We have united. The heart of America feels the cause of France . . . approves her wisdom; blames her excesses. . . . She feels the same fury in her veins. . . . Can we be indifferent? Is not our fate interlaced with hers? For, O! France, if thy republic perish, where is the honour due to ours? . . . and should France say, United States, your neutrality is not sufficient I expect the junction of your arms with mine. . . .Who is there would not say, It shall be so, you shall have them; our citizens shall arm; they shall attack; our oaks shall descend from the mountains; our vessels be launched upon the stream, and the voice of our war, however weak, shall be heard with yours.[24]

Once more he had returned to his early style of fiery images and sudden, staccato questions between balanced sentences; he aimed to move the people with the same spirit that moved him— a political spirit approaching the religious. Yet, there was caution in his words. Although his speech appeared to be a call to arms in defense of France, he carefully inserted a safeguard: the American will to aid France would probably be sufficient; it would serve to comfort the newest republic in the war with monarchy. He was aware of the ultimate effect of his rhetoric on the frontier audience who would tend to ignore the qualifications and to take the oration as an actual call to arms against the British. In such an event, the government would be forced to send troops west to fight the Indians who were allies of the British and who were harassing the settlers; and the vital interests of the West would be served.

Published in the *National Gazette*, the oration stirred enough attention to be reprinted the same year in New York as the work of "Citizen Brackenridge." It appeared alongside an essay by "Citizen Robespierre."[25] By the following year, however, Brackenridge's zeal had abated as a result of the foment in the ultrademocratic societies of Western Pennsylvania. Their violent talk and conduct endangered the Union itself; Brackenridge shuddered at the thought of revolution.

Occurring in his forty-fourth year, the Whiskey Rebellion was the most harrowing crisis in a crises-ridden life. Despite Brackenridge's desperate efforts to remain aloof, the vortex drew him into the very center of events. According to his son's account,

> He had defended the twelve individuals indicted for tarring and feathering an exciseman of the name of Graham; and was employed in the "great case" of the seventy distillers who were prosecuted for not entering their stills according to law. A popularity of this kind no doubt led to some inconvenience as it in some measure identified him with opinions and movements which he did not always approve.[26]

On the pretext of seeking legal advice, each side attempted to obtain Brackenridge's support by coercion. Drawn at last into the public meetings, he imagined that violence might be avoided through guidance; and he allowed himself to serve on committees for this purpose. As he had so boldly announced to Washington, neutrality was impossible. Either he was with the insurrectionists, or he was against them. With his life threatened, he appeared to be in agreement with their proposals. This pretext permitted time for reasoning with them, for delaying, and sometimes for averting violence. When the rebellion dissipated with the advance of the New Jersey troops, he found himself the sworn enemy of the rebel leaders but ironically the symbol of the insurrectionists in the minds of the advancing army. Moving westward, the troops slashed and bayoneted the bushes, calling them "Brackenridge."

Quickly, he printed a handbill explaining his position. He sent it out for distribution to the rank and file, but only a few found their mark. As the advancing militia drew near, he contemplated flight, not trusting the officers' ability to restrain their men. He thought of taking refuge with the Indians, but after several sleepless nights he determined to stand firm. His mind sought solace in the classics; from Plutarch's *Lives* he found the courage to await assassination, if that were to be his fate. Waiting, he put his papers in order and wrote a sketch of his conduct to clear his name in the event of his murder. Neither assassinated nor held for treason, Brackenridge expanded the sketch into a narrative called *Incidents of the Insurrection in Western Pennsylvania in the Year 1794.* He hoped to show how he had been drawn unavoidably into the swirl of activity, and how he had maintained a consistent and patriotic role of mediator.

V *Tree of Liberty*

Although he was in the thickest of political struggles almost to the end of his days, Brackenridge tried to pursue the separate peace with society which he had declared for himself in the last days of the Rebellion. Shunning all political involvement, he followed the advice he had given to William Findley—the cobbler should stick to his last. Brackenridge enjoyed a period of comparative tranquility in which he wrote, read, and reconstructed his law practice. In a short time his eloquence and learning, according to his son's "Biographical Notice," "gave him the first practice as an advocate, so that lucrative business was rather forced upon than sought by him." Most lucrative was his arrangement with Eastern merchants to collect money owed them by Western customers. Moreover, the nature of this law practice allowed a good deal of time for writing. By 1797 he had completed the fourth volume of *Modern Chivalry*, but in a state of mind quite at odds with the spirit of light and amusing satire that had been established in earlier volumes. He looked upon the writing itself as a tonic: ". . . these things are sometimes the offspring of a mind far from being at ease; on the contrary, it is to get ease and allay pain," he says at the beginning of the fourth volume. "The early paroxysm of deep grief may be incompatible with playful fancy; but gradually and insensibly the heart-ache may be cheated of its sensation. . . . The mind is prevented from corroding or gnawing upon itself."

Perhaps this reawakening of his reflective senses caused him also to notice his son. Henry Marie had been living with a French family in Louisiana since 1793, ostensibly to learn the French language, but more probably because of certain objections raised by the new Mrs. Brackenridge. Returning in the company of General James Wilkinson in October, 1796, the boy was filled more with terror than love. As the river boat neared Pittsburgh, he became more and more apprehensive of his father. When the artillerymen at Fort Pitt sighted the general's boat, they alerted the town by booming out a military salute. Brackenridge, however, was not at the dock. Henry Marie found his father "sitting in his office, unmoved by the uproar which had disturbed the whole village."[27] Frightened at the severe aspect of his father and his first words, "Well, boy, can you read French?" the boy only stammered. Now Brackenridge took charge of his education, assuming personally the instruction in English and Latin. Among the works in English was *Modern Chivalry*, and the father's austerity collapsed for joy when he found his son unable to suppress his laughter at the antics of Teague O'Regan.

Through these few years of political retirement, Brackenridge maintained his critical attitude toward former opponents and personal enemies. By 1798, his opposition to Federalist theory and practice had solidified, but the opinion of his fellow Westerners had shifted toward support of the Federalists. According to his son, "But fifty Democrats [anti-Federalists] could be mustered in Pittsburgh, and not all these were entitled to put a ticket into the ballot box."[28] Under these conditions, Brackenridge reentered politics as a Jeffersonian Democrat. He was the founder and leader of the party in Western Pennsylvania. After a vituperative campaign in which he was severely denounced by the *Pittsburgh Gazette,* he lost the race for the State Assembly but managed to win some support for Albert Gallatin, the party's successful candidate for Congress, and for Thomas McKean, the party candidate for governor, who also won. As a reward for his efforts, he was appointed a judge of the Supreme Court of Pennsylvania.

The appointment did not suppress his political activity. Before leaving for the East, Brackenridge pursued a personal war against the newspaper which he had helped to organize. In opposition to the *Pittsburgh Gazette,* he undertook a new journalistic venture that would be the voice of the Jeffersonians in the West. He called it *Tree of Liberty,* and in it he published his own vituperations against John Scull's "blackguard journalism." Scull responded with a sensational exposé of the newly appointed judge on a drunken spree. The *Gazette* was indignant at learning that "a Supreme Judge and sapient philosopher too, will so far lose sight of the reverence due to himself—to his station—and society, as to be seen almost 'stark naked' and nearly 'stark mad' from too much tipple in the face of open day."[29] Brackenridge was attacked also as the "President of the Jacobin Society . . . Biographer of the Insurgents . . . Auctioneer of Divinity, and Haberdasher of Pronouns."[30] And, because he had hired a Jewish editor for the *Tree of Liberty,* "Brackenridge of late seems to have a hankering after the Jews. . . . Like his friend Jefferson the philosopher and the *Roques* of France. . . . That he should turn *Jew* in his old days and build him a synagogue in his own ground, surprises nobody . . . if in one of his crack-brained magazines Hugh has submitted to the *Knife* of his High Priest, is it expected that every man, woman and child will do the same? Are we all to be circumcised without benefit of clergy?"[31] David Bruce, a fellow Scotsman, also chimed in tune with the criticism:

> . . . when a BRACKENRIDGE does shift
> The Muses wail.
>
> What think ye did the Musie say?
> "My bairn," quoth she,
> Your brither Brack has agane gley
> Alas! Wae's me![32]

Bruce, keeper of a country store near Pittsburgh, had written a number of poems defending the Federalists, and Brackenridge had responded in the same dialect. The exchange, however, softened his will to argue and carried him to memories of boyhood among the Scots of the Barrens. In a reflective mood he announced to David Bruce, "But I maun bid you now farewell. . . . Am ganging frae this thoroufare."[33]

The excited Federalists were not about to let him depart without a final bitter thrust. Anticipating his departure, the *Gazette,* which had disintegrated into a mere mouthpiece, devoted the entire issue of September 12 to crude satire and vilification of the new Supreme Court Justice. Now that he could afford it, Brackenridge preserved his mood, condescending to respond in the manner of a man brushing off an annoyance. With the detachment of Gulliver, he saw himself as "a traveller in the Island of Borneo . . . with a thousand monkeys leaping and chattering amongst the trees, and incommoding the Caravan by the fall of excrement."[34] Finally, he advised his Western brethren, "There are two things which money cannot give, instant growth to trees, or immediate refinement to manners. These are both the result of time and cultivation."[35]

Incensed, the Western Federalists capitalized on any vague strand of gossip in order to defame Brackenridge. They recirculated the story of his drunken spree, adding such detail as the amount and kind of liquor consumed at each inn along the route to Pittsburgh. When Mrs. Brackenridge, who was not politically astute, opened a letter from Jefferson that had arrived in her husband's absence and showed it to a visitor, the Western Federalists were able to generate gossip that carried all the way to Washington. The letter merely gave an account of the Vice-President's tie vote with Aaron Burr for the presidency. Although the correspondence could hardly be used to impugn Brackenridge directly, it could be employed most effectively against the Vice-President at that moment. ". . . whoever knows Judge Breckenridge," said the *Washington Federalist,* ". . . and all the group of *virtuous opposers,* as they call themselves, in this country, from Tom Tinkerdown to Tom M'Kean—why then, he will probably know the confidential friends of Tom Jefferson, that's all!"[36] Apologizing to Jefferson for the possible embarrassment caused him, Brackenridge promised to postpone his move from Pittsburgh at least until the vote for the presidency was settled. The Republican cause required his residence in Western Pennsylvania even though it was a place of "vigilant calumny" against him and his family. After the election of Jefferson, Brackenridge wanted no more battling.

VI *The Private World of Judge Brackenridge*

Settled in Carlisle, Pennsylvania, Brackenridge began to doubt the wisdom of Jefferson's policies, particularly those relating to judicial reform. Again he found himself opposing popular opinion. The general distrust of educated persons, prevalent in the West, had come to focus on lawyers and judges. This attitude was abetted by Jefferson's own attitude towards the judiciary: "The greatest object of my fear is the Federal Judiciary. That body, like gravity, ever acting, with noiseless foot, unalarming advance, gaining ground step by step, and holding what it gains, is engulfing insidiously the special governments into the jaws of that which feeds them."[37]

Hatred of the judiciary ultimately brought about proceedings against three justices of the Supreme Court of Pennsylvania. The proceedings grew out of a contempt of court sentence against a Philadelphia merchant, Thomas Passmore. A lower court had favored the merchant in a claim against an insurance company. When the insurers filed an exception to the case with the Supreme Court, Passmore posted a scurrilous note about them in a coffee house, an action which the Supreme Court judged to be contemptuous. Passmore's sentence—fifty dollars and one month in jail—stirred public indignation and resulted in the impeachment charges. If Brackenridge had been sitting at the time of the events named in the charges, there would have been four impeached justices. He did, however, take part in the final hearing of the case and concurred in the sentencing of Passmore. Consequently, he assumed an equal share in the offenses alleged against his fellow justices, and he volunteered to have his name placed among those impeached.

Although the House committee could not accept this offer, the members interpreted his absence from the bench as a neglect of duty and called for a resolution asking the governor to remove Judge Brackenridge from office. Informed by the committee that its resolution was in effect a command, Governor McKean replied that the state constitution specified "might remove," which in this instance meant "won't." In part owing to Brackenridge's support of his colleagues, the judges were acquited. These proceedings and the attitude of the nation provided the impulse for Part Two of *Modern Chivalry*, which began as a satire on the "blackguard press" but changed after the first few chapters to lengthy arguments in favor of the judiciary and the common law.

Though he attempted satire the rest of his life, adding the last touches to *Modern Chivalry* the year before he died, Brackenridge was now attuned to the reflective mood. In 1806 he collected his available poems and essays into a volume entitled *Gazette Publications*. Then he occupied himself collecting essays from American journals for a book called *Spirit of Public Journals: or Beauties of American Newspapers for 1805*. This work may have been the start of an annual series which the author abandoned upon further reflection. The collection demonstrates only that his concern for American journalism was abiding. Between 1805 and 1814 he worked on a far more significant collection, his *Law Miscellanies*.

Several times in Part Two of *Modern Chivalry*, he mentions his more severe studies, his law tracts. After the election of 1805 assured survival of the common law in Pennsylvania, Brackenridge undertook a study aimed at revising it by excising the archaic features and by adapting the remainder to a democratic society. The results of this work are the ingredients of *Law Miscellanies*, which he considered a substantial contribution to American jurisprudence. This opinion was shared at least by Horace Binney, who wrote reports on cases before the Supreme Court from 1807 to 1814.

Experience had diminished Brackenridge's hopes of "Rising Glory" and of a new cultural empire in the West. There remained in him a sedate desire for order in the democracy as it was, a desire for peace and proper laws, for mere safeguards. Ultimately, the law and the force behind it won the people's respect. Surely his tone was resigned when he advised his son, "The profession of the law is the road to honor and preferment in this country."[38] Yet he "despised the law," according to Horace Binney, who observed him in the Supreme Court for seven years: "He once said to me as I was standing by his chair on the bench, "Talk of your Cokes and Littletons, I had rather have one spark of the ethereal fire of Milton than all the learning of all the Cokes and Littletons that ever lived."[39] David Paul Brown, another lawyer of the time, noted, "Judge Brackenridge . . . was reserved and misanthropic. . . . He seemed to shun social or convivial scenes, and to hold a communion only with himself . . . [he] created a world of his own."[40]

This private world was becoming more and more inviolate. At home, his inwardness was little disturbed by visitors except for a few literary friends. The Brackenridges neither dined out nor invited guests to dinner. The singular home activity was study. Three children had been born to Sabina and Hugh Henry, and they were subjected to the same discipline as Henry Marie. At fourteen, the older boy was translating Longinus and Xenophon; at six, the younger boy was mastering Latin and French; and, at three, the youngest Brackenridge, a girl, was reading the newspaper.

Outwardly, Brackenridge seemed to have lost all social awareness. On the bench in Philadelphia and on circuit, he wore a rusty black coat, according to David Brown, and his waistcoat and shirt were almost the same color. Even in the coldest weather he sat with his breast exposed, his beard unshaven, his hair uncombed, his "cravat twisted like a rope." Often he sat in judgment among the most distinguished jurists of the time with his boots off and his feet propped on the desk. After seeing him charge a jury in his bare feet, Horace Binney claimed that Brackenridge owned no stockings. Although his countenance was severe—black, deep-set eyes; mouth sunken from loss of teeth; sallow, wrinkled skin—his conversation, even on the most serious subjects, was permeated with "merriment or ridicule."

Disappointed in his aspirations for a golden age for all men, he valued the knowledge stored within himself, for use in his private world. In *Modern Chivalry,* he had asked:

> "Why is it that I am proud and value myself among my own species? It is because I think I possess in some degree the distinguishing characteristic of a man, a taste for the fine arts; a taste and characteristic too little valued in America, where a system of finance, has introduced law of unequal wealth; destroyed the spirit of the common industry; and planted that of lottery in the human heart."[41]

Remembrance

The "lottery" that had grown in the heart of America need never infringe upon his ideal America envisioned in "Rising Glory." In his private world he could dwell in the spirit of past aspirations, and often he could float back to visit his native Scotland. His son recorded, "My father had a curious collection of the Scottish poets from Jones . . . down to Burns. . . . A perfect enthusiast in everything that related to Scotland, although but five years old when he left that country."[42]

Returning to Pittsburgh on circuit duty after a ten-year absence, Brackenridge read "by chance" Walter Scott's "Lady of the Lake." Thirty years ago, he had come there, to the West, to advance it in literature as well as action. His failure to achieve his dream—to at least express the spirit and beauty of the land at the headwaters of the Ohio—mingled in his sensibilities with Scott's success in romantically portraying the Loch Katrine country. The swelling nostalgia finally spilled into the poem "An Epistle to Walter Scott," which revealed the private world of Judge Brackenridge.

In summing up the life of his father, Henry Marie Brackenridge wrote: ". . . Such was Hugh Henry Brackenridge, a man but imperfectly appreciated in his own day, because like others of original cast of intellect, he was ahead of the age, but whose fame is destined to increase, as it becomes more removed from the times in which he lived."[43] The prophecy of fame came true in an ironical way. It was not his lucid style, his brilliant wit, his great learning, or his literature, but the eccentric personality of Judge Brackenridge that people remembered. He became a part of the frontier legend. Pennsylvania historian Leland Baldwin includes him among the picturesque actors who staged "the pageant of the growth of [our] civilization. . . . Most of us have heard vaguely of Johnny Appleseed, Mike Fink, Simon Girty, Judge Brackenridge, and the Whiskey Rebels."[44]

The legend is a caricature of Brackenridge as a judge, a role he filled with evident incongruousness; the caricature was used to describe Brackenridge as late as 1950:

He was tall, "bent in the shoulders," with a facetious turn of humor that was often at variance with his judicial functions. Careless in dress, often owning only one suit of clothes and no stockings, he was not above kicking off his boots while on the bench and delivering his charge to the jury with bare feet propped on the bar of justice. Once he was seen riding naked through the rain, with his one suit of clothes folded under the saddle, for, he explained "the storm, you know, would spoil the clothes, but it couldn't spoil me." Yet this same backwoods political philosopher wrote commentaries on Blackstone, entertained Philip Egalité in his home and was of sufficient stir in the world to have his portrait painted by Gilbert Stuart.[45]

Perhaps the strength of this reputation has contributed to the general neglect of Brackenridge's literary work and has obscured his place in American literary history.

CHAPTER 4

Writings of the Revolution

THE CRUDE AND OBSTREPEROUS satires Brackenridge
wrote at Princeton render the swelling resentments of Tories
and of English acts—feelings soon to burst into open revolution.
In one of the satires, a Tory named Spring is mentally stumped
by a "den of wicked boys and scribbling men." His immediate
reaction is given as typical: "well then I'll challenge them to
fight . . . put a stop to Whiggish writing/By roaring, snoring,
swearing, fighting." In another, the grievances are quite specific:

> . . . God knows
> I wrote some dirty things in Prose,
> Yes, I remember. T'was in Boston
> I put some tawdry rhimes a post-on
> About the Stamp Act they were written,
> How we were by Europeans bitten.

And on a visit to Philadelphia, a student seeks out a coffeehouse
where he could enter the political dialogue that was apparently
the rage of the time:

> First to the coffee house he went
> And enter'd into learn'd discourses
> In which his judgment's like a Horse's.
> There, after many a wretched blunder,
> He shut his mouth and so knocked under.

To Brackenridge, ignorance is clearly the enemy, not simply of
democracy, but of political independence.

Brackenridge began writing in the traditions of eighteenth-
century English literature. It was primarily a social literature
that relied on Greek and Roman models for guidance. A major

subject was the political transition from monarchy to people's rule. In England, the problem concerned the people's right to rule; in America, the problem abruptly changed to the development and qualifications of a people who would rule. Because Brackenridge pursued the American problem, he produced a literature that imitated his English models in form only.

In England, allusion to Greek and Roman art and thought was largely motivated by a desire to seek perfection through imitation. In Brackenridge's dream of America, represented in his early poems, the classical allusions are intended to inspire emulation. Perfection is for the entire society, all the population; and the character of this perfection remains to be discovered. The problem of educating everybody appears at the very beginning of his work. Education is the prime requirement for success of the democratic experiment. This fundamental idea fades, however, in his political discourses to the troops and in his Revolutionary dramas. These inflammatory pieces were intended to work the blood into action. Characteristically, however, he could not accept the people's rhetoric. In the Revolutionary dramas, he neutralizes his effects with unabashed attempts to put something of great art into situation pieces, and his art is taken mostly from *The Iliad*.

His poems, dramas, and sermons, whether inspired by ideas of independence or by the need to win the war, are all orations. They either celebrate the future or persuade men to act. At the end of the period his work reveals a general weariness with the war and an impatience to get on with the democratic experiment. The *United States Magazine* is one of the nation's earliest efforts to establish rather than assert literary independence; on its pages Brackenridge demonstrates with essay, story, and poem what the others were still talking about. The stirring oratory is replaced with the calmer questions of social and individual experience.

I *Rising Glory and Divine Revelation*

Before the Revolution, most colonial writers confined their impulses for independence to literary competition with English authors. A notable example is John Trumbull. In the preamble to his *Essay on the Uses and Advantages of Fine Arts* (1770), he states: "This land her Steele and Addison shall view,/The former glories equalled by the new." In the "Rising Glory of America," Brackenridge and Freneau refer to themselves not only as "American sons," but also as "we the sons of Britain," apparently meaning that they are American sons of Britain. The glory that will rise, however, is all American. The urge for literary independence is the major impulse behind the poem, and it clearly precedes the urge for national independence.

After the Revolution, a rash of American epics appeared, including the eleven long books of Timothy Dwight's *Conquest of Canaan* (1785) and Joel Barlow's *Vision of Columbus* (1787), which was reworked into *Columbiad* (1807). With obvious hindsight, these proclaimed the manifest destiny of America. Although "Rising Glory" did not foresee political separation, it was the only pre-Revolutionary epic that envisioned America's destiny and its dream.

Not a great achievement when compared with the poems of Virgil and Milton that inspired it, "Rising Glory" is, however, a significant work. It embodies the dream of the new world through a rehearsal of its heroes and of the character and fate of its people—Columbus, Cortez, Pizarro, the Indians, and the Colonists; its promise of agriculture and commerce; and the glorious culture destined for the West. The poem preserves the American mood, thought, and hope that lived on the eve of the Revolution for independence—and all that this Revolution has implied in human history.

In spite of stylistic awkwardness, which is common in early work of most poets, and the burden of allusions to Greece and Rome, common in eighteenth-century literature, "Rising Glory" occasionally rewards the modern reader with fresh pleasure. Most rewarding perhaps is the perception of the poet's classical effort to control the poem's exaggerated images and intoxicated ramble. It is a welding of all the poet's passions—politics, classical literature, oratory, and writing—into a declaration of his life's purpose, which is identical with America's. Though to his son he "confessed that on his part, it was a task of labor, while the verse of his associate flowed spontaneously," the parts written by Freneau are no more moving nor less awkward than those composed by Brackenridge.[1] It is the reader's perception of this "labor" that muffles the ring of the august tones. Today not even an orator of such polish as the young Brackenridge could compensate for the gross stuffing of new-epic qualities nor for the excessive length and repetition of "Rising Glory." For example, the speakers, Eugenio, Leander, and Acasto, repeat the same materials with varying emphasis:

EUGENIO

We see the states
And mighty empires of the East arise
In swift succession from the Assyrian
To Macedon and Rome; to Britain thence
Dominion drove her car, she stretch'd her reign,
O'er many isles, wide seas, and peopled lands.
Now in the West a continent appears;
A newer world now opens to her view.

LEANDER

And here fair freedom shall forever reign.
I see a train, a glorious train appear,
Of patriots plac'd in equal fame with those
Who nobly fell for Athens or for Rome
The sons of Boston. . . .

ACASTO

This is thy praise, America, thy pow'r,
Though best of climes, by science visited,
By freedom blest and richly stor'd with all
The luxuries of life. Hail happy land,
The seat of empire, the abode of kings.[2]

After describing the American inheritance—the continent's beginnings, struggles, heroes and people—the poem points history at last toward man's glorious fulfillment on these shores:

The final stage where time shall introduce
Renowned characters, and glorious works
Of high invention and of wond'rous art
Which not the ravages of time shall waste

> Till he himself has run his long career;
> Till all those glorious orbs of light on high,
> The rolling wonders that surround the ball,
> Drop from their spheres extinguish'd and consum'd
> When final ruin with her fiery car
> Rides o'er creation, and all nature's works
> Are lost in chaos and the womb of night.

All these are original Brackenridge lines. Surprisingly, the verses reveal an awareness of the English graveyard poets but not of the fomenting revolution against a "seat of empire" and "abode of kings." Rather than a political ideal, the Brackenridge lines look forward to a commerce that is profuse, and they "Bid fair science smile." Those of Freneau speak of a rural reign and of no longer shedding blood "For metal buried in a rocky waste."

The epic-like blank verse, imitating the grand style of Milton, was repeated by Brackenridge three years later in "Poem on The Divine Revelation." At that time he apologized: "it may be objected that an imitation of the poet Milton may be traced through the whole performance, though the author has not been able to attain to anything of the spirit of that immortal bard."[3] The spirit of "Divine Revelation" is not of divine glories, lost or regained, but of the golden age dawning for colonial America; and the appropriation of Miltonic grandeur was an attempt to bring something of heaven to earth. The mundane echo of this spirit, without Miltonic grandeur, was heard from Thomas Paine: "America is the theatre where human nature will soon receive its greatest military, civil, and literary honours."[4]

In the preface, Brackenridge apologized not only for the extreme imitation of Milton but for his handling of the theme itself. The religious theme, he indicated, arose not out of deep spiritual experience, but out of a practical consideration of his audience, mostly ministerial. The preface stated that "the subject was chosen perhaps happily enough, as the foundation of an exercise in an institution under the patronage of gentlemen distinguished as friends to revelation." His experiences, apparently, had led him into a re-appraisal of his beliefs, capacities, and ambitions. The "Poem on The Divine Revelation" offers some evidence of this re-appraisal. As the Christian spirit proceeds from the Continent to England and to the American shore, it sheds ritual, dogma, and state affiliation:

> Or those who shunning that fell rage of war
> And persecution dire, when civil pow'r,
> Leagu'd in with sacerdotal sway triumph'd,
> O'er ev'ry consciency, and the lives of men,
> Did brave the Atlantic deep and through its storms
> Sought these Americ shores: these happier shores
> Where birds of calm delight to play, where not
> Rome's pontiff high, nor arbitrary king,
> Leagu'd in with sacerdotal sway are known.
> But peace and freedom link'd together dwell,
> And reformation in full glory shines.[5]

But then on the American shore, the Christian spirit, glowing in its nakedness, is revealed to be a social and scientific spirit hardly associated with its origin:

> Thence to those smiling plains where Chesapeak
> Spreads her maternal arms encompassing
> In soft embrace, full many a settlement,
> Where opulance, with hospitality,
> And polish'd manners, and the living plant
> Of science blooming, sets their glory high.

His thought was consistent from these poetic beginnings through his last efforts at Carlisle. Although the "rising glory" and the "divine revelation" dimmed, they were never quite extinguished; they glowed in his private world even after his society ignored them. To Brackenridge, opportunity for the realization of man's potential was at hand in America. If his "Rising Glory of America" rings with the exuberance of Whitman's *Leaves of Grass,* its "yawp" is not barbaric but quite the opposite.

II *Dramas and Sermons*

The Battle of Bunkers-Hill and *The Death of General Montgomery at the Siege of Quebec* are effete. Men are slain in appropriate poses; no blood is seen. The contrast of these set pieces with the brutal images in his sermons to the troops is astonishing until one realizes that the dramas were written at a school in Maryland while the sermons were composed on the battlefield. Yet Brackenridge had in mind realistic experience for his audience, particularly in the *Death of General Montgomery*. In a note to the play he states that he had received firsthand accounts from survivors of the siege: "I have conversed with those who saw the scalps warm from the heads of our countrymen . . . who beheld the fires lighted up . . . and heard, with a soul paining sympathy, the horrid shrieks and gloomy howlings of the savage tribes in the execution of the poor captives."[6] His outrage at British atrocities is intensified in the second play, but his insistence on the grand style and his dependence upon literary allusions dissipate all emotion. In the preface to *The Death of General Montgomery*, Brackenridge stated: "I meddle not with any of the effeminate passions, but consecrate my muse to the great themes of patriotic virtue, bravery and heroism."

Adhering to the unities, both plays tend more to dialogue and oration than to action. In *The Death of General Montgomery*, foreboding exposition, praise of virtue, and damnation of British treachery and Indian savagery substitute for events. The diction is archaic, and all characters speak almost identically. For example, General Montgomery's speech in Act I, Scene 1, reads:

> O Gallant Souls! A sacrifice more rich
> If such should fall, was never offered up,
> On hill or mountain, to the Sacred sense
> Of liberty: not even when Cato died
> At Utica, or nary a Roman brave
> With Noble Brutus, on Phasalia's plain.

This speech sounds no different from MacPherson's in the following scene:

> Sweet Fame, young hero, shall attend thy years,
> And linked in friendship, as we are linked in death
> Our souls shall mount and visit those fair hills
> Where never-dying bards, and heros stray.

The literary inspiration is more clearly Homer than Milton. Hector's domestic motif in *The Iliad*, for example, is repeated in these lines of General Montgomery:

> I fear not death, but yet it gives me pain
> When the soft passion of my soul flows out,
> In sweet rememberance of Amanda's love
>
> . . . .
>
> Yes, Sweet Amanda, soon disjoined in life
> And the connubial cord loos'd and cut off,
> I must resign thee to the will of Heaven,
> The child unborn that in thy womb thou bear'st.
> Its father may not know, may never climb
> The knee paternal, or call forth a smile.

The indebtedness to Homer is again brought out in Bracken-ridge's note to another line in Act II, Scene 1: "This throb of Heart, that bodes of fatality and is not cowardice." The note reads, "It is marked by critics on the poet Homer, that the courage of his favorite Achilles appears . . . from his inconstancy that though it was foretold by the oracle that he was to fall at the siege of Troy, he had the bravery to engage in that expedition." In spite of these strong indications of the model, biographer Newlin finds major sources in Shakespeare's Henry V; another critic finds that *The Death of General Montgomery* leans strongly on Milton.[7]

Despite the inadequacies of the dramas, literary historians have placed both plays among the best representatives of their time. To Moses Coit Tyler, they had "a literary merit so positive and so remarkable as to justify our study of them even on that account alone."[8] Arthur Hobson Quinn found the verse in these plays "flexible and dignified." Professor Quinn states that "Brackenridge's dramas are better than the other revolutionary plays from the point of structure and expression even if they have not the vigor of action."[9]

The sermons, surprisingly, are far more dramatic than the plays. They are flames of patriotism, fueled with biblical allusion but devoid of piety. Filled with rage against the enemy, they fired the troops with every sentiment except that of the Sermon on the Mount:

They [the British] have landed; they have travelled through a part of the adjascent country; they have burned dwelling houses; they have destroyed provisions and the means of life; they have tortured for money those whom they suspected of possessing it; they have driven the peaceful inhabitants from their places of abode; they have violated the chastity of women who fell into their hands; they are bending on and breathing slaughter to the whole state. . . .[10]

Yet the passion is planned, modulated with deliberate thought:

Let our resentment be leveled against their practice and let our execution be stayed on their bodies; but let us spare the soul. Let us wish them spiritual happiness; but let every thought and exercise of mind draw forth itself against their conduct. Let us endeavor to conceive with strength the baseness of their crime; and let us speak to others what he have conceived, so that we may fix the detestation of it beyond a possibility to be erased. This is laudable, for a just and honest indignation against any vice or evil practice is an evidence of virtue.[11]

The sermons are clever devices of analogy, substituting patriotic and civic passions for religious passions. They deal not with God's control of life but with man's. Since men were not born wicked, Brackenridge believed that progress was possible. Very much in line with Emerson's "Self-Reliance," Brackenridge urged all men to realize their potentials—to equate themselves with all the heroes of history.

His purpose is to arouse a fierce hatred against the British, but that nation's glorious achievements are not diminished. He envisaged "Avon . . . where the fair Shakespeare rises to my view." He told the troops how he was "touched with the magic sound of Milton's harp and the lyre of a Gray modulating soft music to my ravished ear. I lift my thought to the noble strains of Pope, and feel the enthusiasm of the bard rushing to my soul [The quality of enthusiasm is seldom attributed to Pope. Perhaps Brackenridge was still thinking of MacPherson, the author of *Ossian.*] . . . the Lockes, the Bacons, and the Newtons that she boasts. . . . I feel a momentary impulse of concern for a country that gave these noble spirits birth." But now this birthplace of nobleness is "infatuated in her councils, and her renown is declining."[12]

In the dark hour when rumors were heard that the French officers leading the Americans had been recalled, Brackenridge finally brought God into his sermons. God was on the American side, "and the Armies of the universe are not sufficient to resist his providence."[13] In 1778 he published six of the sermons, precisely titling them *Six Political Discourses founded on the Scriptures* and adding a prefatory note for the inattentive: "Let not the word *scripture* . . . prevent that general attention to these discourses which they might otherwise receive . . . these discourses are what they pretend to be, of a nature *chiefly political.*" As such, they provide an unusual interpretation of Old Testament actions and personages. "Woe unto them," he cites from Jude: 11, "for they have gone in the way of Cain"; then the sermon strings together all antecedents of the British who have gone this way, including the Pharaohs, the Ahabs, the Alexanders, the Jenghis Khans, the Tamerlanes, the Huns, the Vandals, and the Goths. "I pass them by, and hasten on, for I have an object of greater wickedness in view—an object of such accomplished fraud, perfidy and murder, that every one heretofore mentioned is lost and disappears. I mean him of England—the fierce, cruel, unrelenting, the bloody king of Britain."[14]

A later critic exclaimed, "How Brackenridge could hate!"[15] But his hate is a product of outrage, one engendered by an enormous compassion for human suffering at British hands. His description of the captured troops has an overwhelming appeal of immediacy that suggests the early Hemingway:

We saw them. . . . The legs swollen, and from the ankle to the knee of an equal shape, the belly contracted to the ribs, the eye sunk and hid within the head, the visage narrow, the cheeks fallen to the bone, the voice shrill, feeble, and not to be distinctly heard, the dress ragged and scarcely hanging to the body. Ask one of these what became of his companion whom we see not? He died the first week partly with hunger and partly with cold. He recommended his wife and infant children to God, and his death to be revenged by his country. What became of another whom we see not? He died the second week on board the ships by the badness and, as we suppose, poison of the food which was served to us. He hoped that the God of heaven and the freemen of his country would call the tyrant to account for this. . . .[16]

Unconscious of making art and truly moved to utterance, he was able to approach the effects that he had so blithely assumed could be achieved with the grand language and allusions of his hollow dramas.

III *The United States Magazine*

In the preface to the first edition of *The United States Magazine,* Brackenridge asked, "For what is man without taste, and the acquirement of genius? An Ouran Outan [*sic*], with the human shape, and the soul of a beast." He called the magazine "a repository of history, politics, and literature." It would serve the cause of American literary independence: "We hope to convince them [the British] that we are able to cultivate the *belles lettres,* even disconnected with Great Britain; and that liberty is of so noble and energetic quality, as even from the bosom of war to call forth the powers of human genius, in every course of literary fame and improvement." The magazine would allow "young and rising authors to make trial of their strength without the risk of being checked in the first stages of their progress by ill-natured critics whose knowledge of their person generally excites envy, and disposes them to censure what they themselves perhaps could not equal."

All these purposes were only aspects of a fundamental political ideal which had crystallized at Princeton and which controlled his actions and writings the remainder of his life: "The mechanic of the city or the husbandman who ploughs his farm by the river bank has it in his power to become, one day, the first magistrate of his respective commonwealth, or to fill a seat in the Continental Congress. This happy circumstance lays an obligation upon every individual to exert a double industry to qualify himself for the great trust." The industrious, however, had little time for study. Nor had they access to books. As a literary coffeehouse, the magazine would provide the knowledge required in capsule form and would substitute for the libraries not yet collected. It would provide instruction to brace the mind, "making it capable of judgment," and entertainment that would "unbend it from study and severe application."[17]

The eroded couplets of his pretentious appeal to subscribers "These shall say when thou art seen,/Oh! enchanting magazine," wholly misrepresented his concept. The contents of the early issues were vibrant with the life and thought of a people struggling to become a nation. The variety of material fulfilled his promise of a literary coffeehouse. Each issue contained a chronicle of current events, digesting foreign and domestic news in regular columns. This digest was an innovation later imitated by Freneau in the *National Gazette,* and remains fixed in American journalism. Unlike earlier editors of journals, Brackenridge minimized the stale news from abroad; his columns were focused on events at home. He listed the members of Congress, the capture of ships, and the battles in various parts of the country; and he published a calendar of political events. There were travel articles; useful scientific expositions, such as "Experiments for Destroying the Fly in Wheat"; advice, such as the note "On Keeping Secrets"; recipes; accounts of Indians; letters from contributors; and instructions to free-lance correspondents, such as this: "Elegance of language may, in some cases, be dispensed with, but delicacy of sentiment is in all cases indispensibly to be preserved."[18]

Without editorial comment, he printed significant public documents affecting the life of the citizen. The editor's contributions, which comprised a large portion of the contents, included a lively satire on hard money that revealed the frivolities of the time. The satire attempts to demonstrate that general demoralization of society results from the debased Continental currency, and it argues for a system of hard cash.

A more enduring contribution was his appeal "To Poets, Philosophers, Orators, Statesmen, and Heroes of Antiquity" to come to the aid of the American democracy. Contributors to the journals of the eighteenth century often signed their articles with pseudonyms taken from antiquity, and the assumed name was usually chosen because of similarity in thought and style between the ancient and contemporary authors. In appealing for contributors to *The United States Magazine,* Brackenridge played with intentional ambiguity upon this custom. "To Poets, Philosophers . . . and Heroes of Antiquity" specifies a particular desire for articles bearing on the problem of a double or single legislature. The article reveals his own political perplexity. (This journalistic attitude of unbiased inquiry was unheard of at that time, and it is still more of an ideal than a reality.) Although the subject—the proposed structure of Congress as a one-house assembly unchecked by a senate—was hotly debated, Brackenridge presented it with cool objectivity; he appealed to the reason through a sense of historical distance. The piece also demonstrates his view of journalism as an instrument of education. It imparts a knowledge of cultural inheritance and applies this knowledge to immediate problems.

In "The Establishment of the United States," a series of articles which stopped abruptly after the seventh issue, Brackenridge attempted to rationalize the rebellion by disqualifying the British claim to the land. Actually, he is more interested in justifying the American conscience in taking the land from the Indians. Since his boyhood in York County, where he may have witnessed the Indian cruelties everyone talked about, Brackenridge had considered the native American a savage animal; he scorned the "noble savage" concept from abroad. In the "Establishment of the United States," he relies on biblical authority to sustain his rationale for denying the Indians any rights to the American soil. The land, he argues, belongs to men who will cultivate it, not to those who remain in the state of hunters. In terms of economy, an animal who lives by the hunt requires a vast extent of land. Through cultivation, however, a civilized man requires but little land. Moreover, agriculture allows all men a share of God's bounty. Not only is this argument rational, but it is the very word of God: "And God blessed them, and God said unto them, be fruitful and multiply and replenish the earth, and subdue it." A man, accordingly, has no mandate from God to occupy more land than he can use for his personal needs. To accommodate all men, the soil must be cultivated, which is God's mandate. This argument also denies the British any rights in America since their claim is based on discovery, not on cultivation.

The United States Magazine entertained its audience through reader correspondence; belles lettres, most notably Freneau's poems; an intriguing serialized story by Brackenridge; and town gossip. Among its contributions to American culture, the printing in its columns of Freneau's "Beauties of Vera Cruz" and "House of Night" was most significant. Unfortunately, the finer work was offset by interminable mock heroics, such as "The Cornwalliad," attacking British and American Tories. If such stuffy satire bored the readers, the unintended humor of General

Charles Lee's letter to Miss Franks regaled them. Miss Franks, a Philadelphia belle, had laughed at Lee's green breeches which had been patched with leather. The general had responded with a letter protesting that his breeches were in accord with the smartest fashion. Perhaps through Miss Franks's sense of humor, the letter fell into the hands of the magazine editor. Chagrined to find it in print, Lee promptly apologized in a second letter to Miss Franks, which Brackenridge published in the *Pennsylvania Advertizer*. This letter referred to the "impertinence and stupidity of the compiler of that wretched performance with the pompous title of the Magazine of the United States."[19] When Brackenridge attacked Lee's military conduct, the general, alarmed now, appealed for a congressional hearing to defend himself. Then, in a moment of self-appraisal, he became quite confounded by his over-reaction; at last, he decided to settle the matter personally. One night, Brackenridge's son relates, his father was awakened by a pounding on his door and by an irate voice shouting: "I'll give you as good a horsewhipping as any rascal ever received." Appearing at an upper story window, Brackenridge replied, "Excuse me, General. I would not go down for two such favors."

Although the work of Brackenridge after the Whiskey Rebellion grows reflective, it actually represents a return to this mood, not a beginning. A continuing story in the first seven issues of *The United States Magazine* reveals strains of sensibility and sentiment not usually found in American literature at this time. His second piece of fiction, "The Cave of Vanhest," was written in 1779 at the height of his patriotic fervor and is powered by a drive to escape society, its problems, and attendant wars. The story, an effort to seek meaning in one's personal life, begins in an atmosphere both natural and supernatural. Much in the manner of Poe, the opening establishes the probability that the narrator should find a cave inhabited by a hermit:

> In my younger years I had read much of that romantic kind of writing which fills every mountain with a hermitage so that you can scarcely miss your way in any part of the country but you stumble upon a residence of this kind and discover some old man who when the usual civilities are over tells you a long story of his conflicts with the evils and accidents of life until, sick of the world, he has retired from it to this cell in which alone he has

found happiness. . . . I have been a thousand times disappointed in my expectation and never had the pleasure to descry any mortal of this stamp until lately in a tour through the Jerseys in company with a young gentleman of Philadelphia.

The tone itself brings Poe to mind: ". . . and immediately the door was opened to us by a man in a long white linen robe, who desired us to walk in and be happy, if we could be happy in the Cave of Vanhest." Within the cave, the air is full of expectation. The ornate interior is richly described:

> There stood a bed at one angle of the cave with a set of hangings of the finest chintz, variegated with a thousand flowers of the springing year. At another angle was placed [a] buffet replenished with china cups of every shape and dimension. The floor was covered with a very rich carpet whose variety of figures resembled that which Themistocles alluded to in his conversation with the king of Persia. . . . The neat but small mahogany table that stood upon it was that around which we sat down to breakfast and which supported a set of china cups depicted with the tops of the jonquil, also a silver tea urn of the most original construction.

Although Vanhest is estranged from society, he wishes to know about the life of his visitor and the battle of Monmouth from which he has fled; but the hermit will not tell his own story. Instead, it is revealed through the narrator's observations.

The hermit has attained happiness with his family by removal from society, although he is aware of its movements and thoroughly educated in its culture and history. Sustained by sweet plums from the trees he himself has planted in the wilderness and by the fine company of his daughters, the hermit emerges as the prototype of the ideal pioneer; a cultured individual, he has created his own life in the wilderness and fostered a self-sustaining social unit. His family is not only cultured and beautiful but also protective of the weak, as symbolized by the care his daughter gives to a half-witted servant who suffers an injury. Comparisons between the harmony and beauty in the cave of Vanhest and the disrupted, destructive life of society at war cause the narrator to review his own ambitions with all their frustrations. He sees that he had confused his former loves—Miss Theology, then Miss Muse, then Miss Law—

with his ambition. Now his love will be the ladies of the cave. The story presents the author's first painful realization that perhaps the muses had not favored him after all. The basic theme is a search for the beautiful life; and, though the story begins in a mood of mystery, it quickly exchanges this mood for one of nostalgia, of a yearning for personal satisfactions recalled from distant dreams.

These dreams, however, can be realized now, as the hermit realizes them in his symbolic plums:

> "There are," said I, "a great variety of plums in the different soils of America."
> "Yes," replied the hermit, "and some of them very fine; equal, if not superior to any to be found in Europe or the more eastern countries. This plum, which is of the red cherry kind, is excellent to be eaten from the tree and suits very well for sweet meats. I have been told there are fine plums on the creeks to the westward."

As in "Divine Revelation," the most glorious definition of man would be fulfilled in the West. This manifest destiny is no fanciful idea but a reality occupying the very center of Brackenridge's thought.

Perhaps it is significant that the "Cave of Vanhest" and "The Establishment of the United States" end in the same issue. By the eighth issue, the vigor of the magazine had noticeably dissipated. Apparently the editor had lost interest. The quality of the articles in the remaining numbers deteriorated and the variety diminished. The last few issues were filled with state constitutions. Yet, buried in the final number, that of December, 1779, was an article of fresh significance in the immediate future of the nation, "On Enfranchisement of the Negro." In it Brackenridge threw an early light upon the coming struggle: "It casts a shade upon the face of this country that some of those who cultivate her soil are slaves." He blamed Calvinistic predetermination of pain and misery for the non-elect as the ugly instrument used to justify slavery, and he proposed a solution: "Cast out the bond-woman and her son"—out into new freedom. He proposed to give them the land in the wilderness beyond the Ohio which the Indians had forfeited through their hostilities.

Aimed at stimulating ordinary men to study in order to understand their democratic actions, *The United States Magazine* exemplified an idealistic function of journalism in a democratic society. According to Professor Frank Luther Mott, "it was probably the most brilliant performance of the whole period."[20] Aside from any brilliance it may have displayed, the magazine served the cause of American literary independence because it was an action instead of another complaint. Until the Revolution, American magazines were imitations of English publications; even Benjamin Franklin acknowledged his own *General Magazine* to be "an imitation of those in England."[21] And William Bradford proudly asserted that the success of English magazines encouraged him to try "a work of like nature in America . . . [so] that the Parliament and people of Great Britain may be truly and clearly informed of the constitution and government of the colonies."[22]

CHAPTER 5

Modern Chivalry and Other Satires

IN SPITE of his giant's share of misfortune at the hands of the people, Brackenridge never satirized with Swift's bitterness nor with Butler's malignity. In his adaption of Cervantes' picaresque form for *Modern Chivalry* he rendered an aspect of the American society in its essence, as Cervantes rendered an aspect of the Spanish national character. Brackenridge's satire was intended not only to ridicule but also to assert. Consequently, this work differs from its English models in openly stating ideals and in displaying evils. His assertions tend to dilute the moral indignation. *Modern Chivalry* does not conform, therefore, to the definition of great satire advanced by Professor Louis I. Bredvold: "Good satire may be withering, it may be dark anger, it may be painfully bitter, but it cannot be great satire without having at its core, a moral indignation."[1] The satire of Brackenridge is, at core, moral instruction. Moral indignation, Professor Bredvold has explained, is achieved through "understanding of the fellow feeling with which the satirists sustained one another." Brackenridge, a lone satirist on the frontier, had old-world literature but no fellows to sustain his feelings. Thus, he could not depend on the group to perceive his positive meanings. To be effective, he had to teach the moral that was being abused. As a result, the bite of his satire weakened.

The business of a satire, states Juvenal in the *First Satires,* is to "laugh and bite"—to achieve a combination of adverse criticism and of wit. According to Dryden, satire must also be indirect: "There is a vast difference betwixt the slovenly butchering of a man and the finesse of a stroke that separates the head from the body and leaves it standing in its place."[2] The satires that Brackenridge called "Hudibrastics" were surely "the sloven-

ly butchering of a man." His target was his political adversary,
William Findley:

> What though he wished to damn the motion
> Of opening passage to the ocean
> By Mississippi; and what's more
> Of making roads to her own door
> And voted with a stubborn will
> Against the Pittsburgh County bill.[3]

Aside from awkward syntax, these couplets do not insinuate, as
Dryden demands; and they ill accommodate the topical subjects
that the author stuffed into them. Pope, taking advantage of the
couplet structure, often balanced one line against the other and
thus achieved the sharpness of concise antithesis. Brackenridge,
ignoring the structural advantages, used his couplets to explain
his protests. Probably he committed his complaints to the couplet
form because he wished to imply a sense of order, of reasoning,
and even of wit found in the English counterparts; and perhaps
he imagined this sense would emphasize the lack of such qualities
in demagogue William Findley, the object of the satire.

The satire of Brackenridge was a call to action written from
within the stream of events and fully understood only in the
freedom of prose, not in the restraining form of Butler's mock
heroics. In prose also Brackenridge failed to match the effects
of his models. Swift's prose maintained the indirectness and concision necessary to satire. Swift did so by fictionalizing, or rep-
resenting the topical in metaphors, as exemplified in "A Modest
Proposal," *A Tale of the Tub,* and *The Battle of the Books.* When
Brackenridge fictionalized in prose, he invented characters to
view and to experience events, but the events were not given
metaphorical representations. They were real events. Yet they
were not mere topicalities as in his verse satire. He selected the
events to represent the essence of democratic experience. As
direct representations, however, they were closer to history than
to fiction.

I *"Father Bombo's Pilgrimage"*

Only in his first story, the picaresque "Father Bombo's Pilgrimage," does Brackenridge attempt metaphorical representation in the style of the master. Ludicrous as it may be, this first

groping towards the Swiftean manner displays a robust, boisterous humor that is always on the verge of breaking through
the author's control, and thus it imparts the feeling of the
baroque. This feeling emerges from much of his later prose,
most obviously from *Modern Chivalry.*

Although his hopes of a cultured democracy—a nation of
educated gentlemen—dimmed through the personal defeats of
his life, nothing could extinguish them. "Father Bombo's Pilgrimage" emits sparks of these abiding hopes. It reveals that,
even before his celebration of "The Rising Glory of America,"
Brackenridge was absorbed with problems of maintaining cultural values in a democracy and with the relations of these
values to democratic success. With wit and learning, Bombo
extricates himself from one difficulty after another. Most significant is the fact that all the human barriers share the traits of
ignorance and superstition.

Bombo, the traveler to Mecca, is taken prisoner on a French
vessel; when it is attacked on the high seas, he is imprisoned
aboard an Irish privateer. The prisoner roguishly assumes an
Irish brogue and impresses his new captain with his display of
knowledge. The captain gives him the run of the ship until the
sailors begin to fear him as a wizard; then he is bound in the
ship's hold. When a storm arises, the ignorant sailors blame the
wizard, as in mythic literature. Thrown overboard in a barrel,
Bombo washes to a North Ireland shore, still confident of his
own powers to triumph over all obstacles on his way to Mecca.

Humor is sustained through the conflict between Bombo's
knowledge and wit and the ignorance of his captors, whose
minds are webbed in superstition. "Change but the name," the
motto reads, "the story's told of you." Knowledge, wit, and courage move the superstitious and the dull to respectfulness; but the
seamen respect Bombo only as a mysterious power controlling
their fate. When the power cannot ward off the storms of nature,
they throw it overboard. In this action the seamen symbolize all
ignorant men who grasp their freedom with a licentious spirit—
and cast away their inheritance of culture and their respect for
wisdom which are fundamental prerequisites for success in the
new democratic venture.

"Father Bombo's Pilgrimage" anticipates the theme of all the author's satire. Ignorance and freedom of choice continually confront and thwart Bombo, and they become the most outstanding qualities of Teague O'Regan in *Modern Chivalry*. In fact, Teague, the generic term for the ignorant Irish immigrant, first appears in "Father Bombo's Pilgrimage." The story also foreshadows elements of his style—the use of dialect, low-level language, exaggeration, and commonplace detail—which became major characteristics in American Western humor. Except for the use of German, Irish, and Scottish dialects, appearing extensively in his later satire, all these elements can be traced to his classical reading. In eighteenth-century England the ancient authors were criticized by Lord Chesterfield and others for describing the common, for employing undignified language, for allowing heroes and heroines to vent violent emotions and even to work with their hands. In the vibrancy and movement of the New World, these characteristics sprouted through the loosely woven pattern of polite society. Thus, even before Brackenridge moved west, where the weave of polite society extruded into mere strands, he was realistically holding the mirror to nature.

II *Modern Chevalier*

On the frontier the mirror reflected crude aspects of human nature which also have counterparts in ancient works. The expanded attitudes of self reflected in *Modern Chivalry* and in the Hudibrastic verse are almost parodies of Homer's heroes. The boasting and amorality of Homer's ancient figures are revived in the frontiersmen who can perform almost any deed in their new freedom. Ironically, they prefer infamous deeds, such as burning a church or an academy, or tarring and feathering the exciseman. Although the parallels might bring the weight of man's history to bear upon contemporary follies, they are far from exact; but they do appear intentional and are inescapable for the alert reader.

The first form of *Modern Chivalry* had been a lengthy Hudibrastic in which Brackenridge had incorporated a foil for the ignorant Traddle. The foil was a modern chevalier, a hazily developed knight errant traveling the countryside and observing

American politics and society. Coming upon the weaver's cabin, the chevalier decides to amuse himself with a

> . . . breed that earth themselves in cellars
> Like conjurors or fortune tellers;
> Devoid of virtue and of mettle,
> A sort of Subterranean cattle
> Of no account in church or state
> Or ever think of being great.[4]

Chiding, he suggests that the weaver make something of himself— perhaps a statesman. They are interrupted by Traddle's wife whose cudgel on the weaver's rump cancels any signs of rising ambition. Resisting a knightly impulse to draw his sword, the chevalier learns that this lowly creature, this Traddle, has attempted politics; and, save for the strength of his wife, he would be the champion of the people. A serious observer then states the theme of the narrative by gently castigating the chevalier:

> It would do service to the state
> If such a noble Knight as you
> Would teach them what they ought to do,
> And give them seasonable lessons
> Respecting such their wide creations
> That on the one hand while they pass
> The ignorant though monied ass,
> So on the other should avoid
> The chusing such amongst the crowd
> As are unqualified, though less
> They may in property possess.

After writing some thirty pages, Brackenridge imagined such lines might comprise an American Hudibras. Years later, he gave this painfully honest explanation for adopting prose in place of Butler's Hudibrastic verse:

> To me the verse of Butler is not less pleasing than the prose of Cervantes: but though in my opinion my verse imitation of that of Butler is not without some felicity of imitation, yet never having been complimented to the same extent by others, I thought proper to change my composition into that of prose; or rather to drop the continuation of it in verse, and take to prose, which was a more humble and might be a safer walk.[5]

Apparently he failed to see that his poetry lacked clarity and rhythm, that the chevalier was a mere shadow of a character, and that the whole did not impart the vigor and the reality its author had experienced. Simply "thinking that it might be more acceptable in prose," he divested his chevalier of conventional trappings and transformed him into Captain Farrago, an educated gentleman at leisure, with the ideals, rationale, and sympathies of Hugh Henry Brackenridge.

Traddle faded into the background, and Teague O'Regan, the Captain's servant, a delightful combination of brash ignorance and ambition, stepped into full view. This portrait of the indentured Irish servant had first glimmered in the author's mind in 1787, while chastising Findley:

> What wonder then that Teague O'Regan
> Like Asteroth, or idol Dagon,
> Should here receive our reverence,
> In spite of Truth and common sense;
> Men in all ages are the same,
> And nature is herself to blame,
> Who has not given to all an eye
> Of Sapience and philosophy.[6]

Later Brackenridge explained the derivation of Teague in this way:

In the winter of 1787, being then of the legislature of Pennsylvania, it was signified to me that I might be put in nomination [for the American Philosophical Society] with several others, that were about to be balloted for, if I thought proper to skin a cat-fish or do something that would save appearances, and justify the society in considering me a man of philosophic search and resources. Enquiring who these might be, that had been nominated, and put upon the list, and not chusing to be of the *batch*, I thought proper to decline the compliment. It was this which gave rise to my ideas of such a candidate as Teague O'Regan for that honour. Some time after this, when delegates were about to be chosen from the country where I resided to frame a constitution for the United States, after the adoption of the federal government, I offered myself for this, as considering it a special occasion; but to my astonishment, and before I was aware, one of Shakespear's characters, Snout, the bellows mender was elected. This led me to introduce Teague as a politician.[7]

III Modern Chivalry

The novel form allowed Brackenridge to round Teague into the first developed character in American fiction and to place him in a real world. The Hudibrastic prototype of *Modern Chivalry* was formed in an abstract region of the author's political thought; but Teague's picaresque adventures carry the reader through the real country from the Western frontier to Philadelphia and back again.

Although the picaresque structure is borrowed from Cervantes' *Don Quixote,* the representations and mood of *Modern Chivalry* are original, arising from the impact of frontier life upon the mind of a trained classicist. The satirical mood approaches the geniality of Horace rather than the severity of Juvenal. Brackenridge ridicules the foibles and follies of frontier life to show the new democrats their shortcomings—their needs for education, refinement, and self-knowledge. Ambition and ignorance are the targets of the satire; success of the democratic experiment depends upon the people's learning.

Captain John Farrago, a gentleman at leisure whose ideas are "drawn from the old school, the Greek and Roman way of looking at things," administers the lessons while his servant, Teague O'Regan, illustrates them. As Farrago and Teague travel to Philadelphia and back, the characters, events, and customs they encounter stimulate the bogtrotter's ambition to rise in the new democracy though he can neither read nor write. With this narrative scheme Brackenridge was able to present a panorama of life in the burgeoning democracy and to demonstrate his critical judgments, many of them still pertinent and stimulating. Pomposity of the erudite, boorishness of the backwoodsman, and effete avarice of the Eastern politician are all pilloried in the embracing portrait of early society in the United States.

The major motif—"let the cobbler stick to his last"—implies no aristocratic concept of fixed stations in life. Through education and application of talents, the cobbler may become more than a cobbler and thus qualify for the broader responsibilities of a statesman. For Brackenridge, education meant a thorough knowledge and understanding of the Roman and Greek worlds.

The theme is introduced in the first episode in which the Captain encounters sportsmen preparing for a race and is "unwilling to impose his horse for a racer; not being qualified for the course." This thesis is then applied to the political scene where a weaver and a man of education are contesting for the people's vote. Inspired by the weaver's incompetence, Teague, whom the author does not describe "because the very name imports what he was," becomes obsessed with ambition to be a legislator himself. Farrago employs all his rhetorical power but cannot dampen the crowd's instant enthusiasm for his illiterate bogtrotter. After the Captain's rhetoric, containing the democratic lesson the author hopes to inculcate, fails to convince the mob, he appeals directly to his servant. He dissuades Teague by illustrating the personal loss he would suffer in public office, the freedoms he would sacrifice, and the ills that would befall him. This scene establishes the pattern for most of the episodes in the novel.

At the beginning, others stimulate Teague's ambition, but it is not long before he can arouse it himself. Upon first acquaintance with Teague, a philosopher proposes to present him for membership to Dr. Franklin's American Philosophical Society. A few evenings later, however, he decides for himself to become a minister to God. The inspiration is a clergyman who stops Teague from attacking an innkeeper's daughter. Before the entire population of the inn, Teague reverses the situation, making the minister the culprit and himself the savior. After Captain Farrago forces Teague to confess and clear the honor of the minister, the bogtrotter conceives for himself the idea that he too could have the honor of being a man of God; and he cleverly suggests to the presbytery that his ultimate ambition was to be a candidate for holy orders, a suggestion most favorably received.

Once embued with ambition, Teague is vulnerable to the schemes of charlatans. He is all for becoming king of the Kickapoos until the Captain dissuades him by exposing the money-making scheme of selling the government fake Indian treaties, made by fake Indian chiefs whose agreements are verified by interpreters—the schemers themselves.

When the occasions arise, the brash illiterate presents himself as a candidate for a university professorship and for the acting and the legal professions. Teague as lover, however, achieves most success; he drives to distraction suitors of breeding who cannot compete with his brogue, his bumptiousness, and his raw sentiments which young ladies mistake as intentional satire of their suitors and as the ultimate in wit. Masquerading as Major O'Regan in Philadelphia, Teague becomes the darling of feminine society. Only the Captain's plotting with fathers and rejected lovers keeps Teague from the fullest enjoyment of his triumphs. At the end of the second volume, he is contemplating a career as a government official, a situation that finally causes the Captain to capitulate. No longer able to withstand popular demand for ignorance in office, Farrago attempts to reduce the evil by educating the bogtrotter for his high position.

In keeping with the covert requirements of satire, Brackenridge's ostensible purpose in writing the novel was to supply a means which would

> fix the English language. . . . It has always appeared to me that some great master of stile should arise, and without regarding sentiment, or subject, give an example of good language in his composition, which might serve as a model to future speakers and writers, it would do more to fix the orthography, choice of words, idiom of phrase, and structure of sentence, than all the dictionaries and Institutes that have ever been made.[8]

For any reader missing the intended irony, the author provided this emphasis: "I shall pay no regard to idea; for it is not in the power of human ingenuity to attain two things perfectly at once." His intention is to impart at least two things at once: first, to demonstrate the minimum requirements for a representative of the people and for democratic people themselves; and, second, to do so with an educated pen. His target is not only politics but all aspects of society contorted by misconceptions of democracy. In the course of the work Brackenridge states his real purpose many times:

> I shall have accomplished something by this book, if it should keep some honest man from lessening his respectability by pushing himself into public trust for which he is not qualified.

> .   .   .   .

> If these strictures shall have the effect to cultivate a sense of honour in our candidates and in our voters, it will be worthwhile to have written this book.

> .   .   .   .

. . . such is the sanguine temperament of the human mind, that who is there that does not think himself equal to any undertaking? This is the moral of the book, and the object of setting the example of the bog-trotter before the people.

The first two volumes were published in Philadelphia in 1792, and a year later Brackenridge published a third in Pittsburgh. This slim third volume of ninety-nine pages was the first literary work published west of the Allegheny Mountains.[9] He hoped his novel would become a "kind of classic," since it was "formed on the model of Xenophon and Swift's *Tale of a Tub* and *Gulliver's Travels*." Its style, he said, was "simple, natural, various, and forcible." The language was also ribald and exaggerated, having emerged from the real life of the American West; but it was not confined to any locale. The style employed in satirizing the backwoods boors and demagogues did not change when the bog-trotter inspired "a kind of Teagomania amongst the females" of Philadelphia, or when the Captain observed the new rich, the demagogues of the East: "in the country, in my route, they would elect no one but a weaver, or a whiskey distiller; and here none but fat swabs, that guzzle wine and smoke segars."

At the conclusion of the third volume, Brackenridge wished that "I could get this book to make a little more noise. Will nobody attack it and prove that it is insipid, libellous, treasonable, immoral, or irreligious? . . . Will nobody speak? What? Ho! Are ye all asleep in the hold down there at Philadelphia?" Literature was produced in New York, in Philadelphia, in Hartford, and in other civilized points of the East. Of course Philadelphians would not listen. What would they hear but the discordance of the roughnecks—their heavy-handed bluster, slapstick, exaggeration, and uncompromising directness? Later, similar noises would sound out of the farther West; but now, while the East proposed to be championing the cause of an independent American literature, its ears were attuned to the accustomed sounds of England and the continent.

Once Brackenridge resumed writing his satire four years later, he did not stop again until the end of his life. Before its completion in 1815, the early volumes of *Modern Chivalry* had become "to the West what Don Quixote was to Europe—a satirical lash to whip the follies of the times and excoriate mendacious ignorance . . . the humorous text of all classes of society."[10] Unfortunately, when the nation's literary focus turned West, it was to a much farther West than the old frontier of the Ohio valley.

The satirical representations of actual events in *Modern Chivalry* serve as exaggerated examples or anecdotes from which morals, ideals, or lessons can be induced. *Modern Chivalry* is structured to emphasize the positive assertions made by the author or his spokesman, Captain Farrago. Its narrative action is subordinated to its expository lessons in democracy. Brackenridge states that this structure is an imitation of nature: "It is so in nature; and why should it not be so represented in the image of her works[?] We have the sage and the fool interspersed in society, and the fool gives occasion for the wise man to make his reflections. So in our book." The fiction of *Modern Chivalry*, then, is but an emphatic technique to introduce unmasked lessons. An excellent storyteller, Brackenridge employed exaggerated narrative illustration as the point of departure in many of his journalistic essays. *Modern Chivalry* can be viewed as a continuing collection of such essays unified through the consistent use of two central characters.

The author kept adding incidents throughout his life; and as he added, the direct lessons smothered the narrative elements. Looking back on his accomplishment, Brackenridge seldom referred to *Modern Chivalry* as fiction. He spoke of it usually in a plural sense, as a collection of "strictures" which "should have the effect to cultivate a sense of honor in our candidates and in our voters." They are "lessons to grown people." In writing them, his "pain of mind is relieved by an abstraction of solid thought." The amusing parts, the narrative elements, are an unwanted chore: "Were it not that I am afraid of . . . losing readers, it would be more agreeable to my own mind to moralize more. But I have not forgot that it is only by means of amusing that I could get readers, or have the opportunity of reaching the public with my lecture."

Modern Chivalry can hardly be considered a novel even in the didactic or picaresque sense because the episodes fail to create a cumulative effect. In *The Rise of the American Novel* Alexander Cowie says, "the term novel must be stretched considerably to accommodate *Modern Chivalry*." Its theme is not developed but repeated or applied in a variety of situations. Although Teague O'Regan and Captain Farrago are given enough roundness to appear real, they are not developed, changed, or revealed through the action; and the other characters are caricatures simply used to illustrate social habits, abuses, and absurdities. The events proceed to no outcome. Claude M. Newlin places the book high among minor American classics primarily because of its essay value, because it "not only throws light on the beginnings of American democracy but . . . also stands as a permanently valid commentary on persistent problems."[11]

Although the light of *Modern Chivalry* is exaggerated, it reveals the substance of early democratic life as well as its problems. Through the exaggeration the reader discerns the reality of the cultured, the ignorant, the rich, and the poor in their daily lives and common places. He sees the statesmen, philosophers, ecclesiastics, Philadelphia belles, frontier gamecocks. He is thrust into the economic and political conditions and experiences the stupidity of the electors, the hypocrisy of the demagogues. He hears a meaningless speech in Congress, witnesses a trial by a jury of ignoramuses, listens to radical political reformers, observes the misuse of Indian appropriations, and battles with the blackguard journalists. He endures the snobbishness and artificiality of the East—and the Western resentment of law, learning, and anything associated with the East.

Attention to scene at the expense of concision permits the author to render the speech, mind, and habit of frontier people, and permits literary historians to include Brackenridge among the earliest local-color writers. In *American Fiction* Arthur Hobson Quinn has observed: "From the days of Brackenridge and Royall Tyler, American novelists have not been unaware of locality. . . . It is a mistake to speak of Bret Harte as though he discovered something new in the fictional treatment of a locality." The characteristics associated with the term "local color"— scenery, custom and mood of a place, moral contrast, exaggerated story and characters, local dialect, provincial nomenclature, adoption of colorful nicknames, vigilante committees, reformers, bungling of justice, farcical legal machinery and electioneering, gamblers and self-righteous ministers, foreigners and queer and cultured Easterners, treacherous Indians and the white man's manipulation of them[12]—these are the elements that flavor Brackenridge's prose satires.

Like the later local colorists, Brackenridge wrote within an atmosphere of rough humor, incongruity, and exaggeration. Like them, he burlesqued his boisterous settings without the painstaking patience and restraint necessary for developing concise form. In no way did his prose contribute to the development of the American novel and short story as art forms; but at least one critic has found that his satire contributed to the direction of the American novel. "Writers like Brackenridge, Irving and Mark Twain . . . [contributed by] interpreting and appraising many varied and important phases of our social history."[13]

In *American Humor,* Constance Rourke attributes the lack of form among the Far Western local colorists to a pervading atmosphere of euphoria. Reaching the Pacific Coast, they imbibed in the spirit of "a final empire and a release. . . . Again, as in the Ohio Valley when wild bands of river boatmen made their loud rejoinders, the idyllic touch receded or was overlaid by a rougher expression. . . . The whole ritual of the pioneer experience was repeated with new intensity." Except for the lack of patriotic bombast, these Far Western writers "In theme, in tone, belonged to the [earlier] frontier." Again the impulse was comic, and the comedy was based on the tradition of social criticism. Artemus Ward and Mark Twain used local lingo as miming techniques with critical purposes, but the "lingo was far less regional than that of . . . an earlier day." Ward used Yankee speech with an overlay and called it Hoosier, "a composite of American speech." *American Humor* concentrates on Petroleum V. Nasby as representative of the attack on abuses, foibles, and follies of the time. His "satirical view of the affairs of the nation," Rourke states, "belonged to the earlier figures." Among these figures, perhaps centrally, stands Brackenridge.

Whether or not Brackenridge directly influenced the Western tall story, his satire is in the same vein. The adventures of Teague O'Regan are actually tall stories. Without the moralizing intervention of Captain Farrago, they would seem as anecdotal as Twain's "Notorious Jumping Frog of Calaveras County." Much of the satire in Western local color is marked by anecdotal rather than story form. The narrative ability of Twain also lay in developing single episodes. According to Alexander Cowie, "He wrote few books that could come even loosely under any classification of the novel, and those few belonged to a looser category of the novel, namely, the picaresque. [He was] weak in the use of traditional elements of the novel—characterization and plot."

IV *Tone and Attitude*

The frequent bitterness in Twain, however, is seldom found in Brackenridge's satire. Twain begins his fiction without any hope for a rising glory of America. If the reader can view the corrupt politicians in *The Gilded Age* as later Teague O'Regans who have more nearly realized their ambitions, he can attribute Twain's caustic tone to the hopelessness of political ideals in his own day, that is, to the defeat of all Brackenridge's democratic instruction.

Teague O'Regan is as innocent as Huck Finn, but his ambitious acts are potentially harmful to society. A fundamental difference between these rogues is their social orientation. Brackenridge employs his rogue to point the reader toward social reform; Twain concentrates on the rogue as an innocent individual faithful to himself in a society that frequently opposes him. Twain ignores concepts of reform or social change. *Huckleberry Finn* emphasizes what is; *Modern Chivalry* emphasizes what ought to be. Brackenridge suffered personal disappointments as severe as Twain's, but his satire still reflects an attitude of hope. It is almost good-natured; indeed, to Claude M. Newlin it is "lacking in fundamental criticism."[14]

Two years after he published *Incidents of the Insurrection,* Brackenridge issued a fourth volume of *Modern Chivalry* (1797). It viewed the same events with a satirical lens. Teague was given his government appointment—that of an excise officer—and Captain Farrago was forced to employ in his place a Scotsman. The new bogtrotter, however, is more highly developed and has theological leanings. He rebels when they meet Teague upon the road. The Captain suggests that his new servant and the new excise officer share a bed at a crowded inn: "Guid deliver me frae sik a prophanation o' the name o' Ferguson as to sleep wi' an excise officer." Teague's reply shows the author's development of realistic technique, of creating similar but differing characters largely through language: "The devil burn me, said he, if I will be often slapeing wid you, you son of a whore, you teef luking vagabon; wid de itch upon your back; I am sure all your country has de itch; and keep scratching and scratching, as if de ware in hell, and could get brimstone for noting; you son o' a whore."

Proud in his new office, the exciseman is quickly leveled by the fate which befell his predecessors. He is tarred, feathered, and driven out. Fearing similar treatment, Captain Farrago does not attempt reasoning with the violent mob, although he had stated his opinions to his servant when stopped earlier on the road: "The law in question is odious and great allowance ought to be made for the prejudices of the people. By soft measures, and mild words, prejudices may be overcome. These appear to be but young men: and rashness is a concomitant of early life. By expostulation we may probably have the good fortune to be able to pass on, without being under the necessity to attempt battery or shed blood." When the militia arrives, the Captain is accused of traitorous acts but is acquitted by an "examiner of sense." As a scientific curiosity, the tarred and feathered Teague is shipped to France. This volume, though written to "get ease and allay pain," is, like the others, free of bitterness.

The tone of Brackenridge's satire, however, can never be taken as congenial. It has little in common with the satire of Washington Irving, who attacked neither individuals nor groups and who sought no direct social progress. Aimed at social change, Brackenridge's satire cannot afford relaxation and therefore cannot acquire Irving's congenial tone. Brackenridge, under constant attack from political enemies, could not indulge in the luxury of self-parody or of kindness toward the demagogues at whom his satire was aimed. The absurdities of American life amused Irving but they threatened Brackenridge.

He depicted his society with a critical eye. One observer of early American literature, Tremaine McDowell, finds that "The only deliberate enemy of excessive expansiveness [of the pathetic] is Brackenridge."[15] Yet this critic sees that Brackenridge shared sympathies with novelists of sensibility. McDowell points particularly to the author's anti-slavery remarks. Actually Brackenridge's sensibilities extend much further. *Modern Chivalry* is touched frequently with sentiment. However, sentiment seldom occupies the focal point of his work, and it is never idealized as in the standard novels of seduction in his time. Both *The Power of Sympathy* (1789) and *Charlotte Temple* (1791), for example, are constructed about the Richardsonian theme of feminine virtue idealized through distress; and in both novels sentiment rages unchecked. In *The Power of Sympathy*, Harrington is a wolf preying on the innocence of the lowly and unprotected Harriet until her unutterably white virtue causes a reversal. Then he becomes the epitome of the true lover who defies parents and life itself. Mrs. Rowson's more popular novel remorselessly condemns its heroine to the tragic fate awaiting all women fallen from virtue however they may have been deceived and however strong their resistance to a second temptation.

The sentiment of Brackenridge is usually checked by one quality that the sensibility writers seldom displayed, an abiding realism. Before the subject of sentimental love is burlesqued in Teague O'Regan's affairs, Brackenridge treats the theme seriously. Searching through Philadelphia for his absent bogtrotter, the Captain is led to a brothel where he encounters a young lady who has fallen through the sin of love and has been unwillingly maneuvered into a prostitute's life. After promising to find a respectable home and livelihood for her, the Captain returns the next day to discover that the girl has killed herself. In the standard sentimental treatment, the girl fallen from virtue could not have tumbled all that way; but, if so great a fall were possible, she certainly would have grasped the last straw, such as the Captain's selfless pledge to find a new home for her. The surprise of her suicide renders the reality of her despair and her extreme cynicism of all men and their words. Such realistic treatment of sentiment is rare in eighteenth-century American letters. According to Tremaine McDowell, "No novelist save Brackenridge showed indebtedness to either Fielding or Smollet, . . . [whose] realism . . . blinded American sentimentalists to their undeniable touches of tearfulness."[16]

V *Style and Thought*

Conscientiously, Brackenridge worked to keep his style from intruding upon the sense. Deploring the prose of Samuel Johnson, whom he called a "literary dunce," he chose to follow the simplicity of Swift, Hume, and Fielding whom he judged as equals in grace and naturalness. Commenting in *Modern*

Chivalry, he found that "nothing could surpass" Swift's definition of style—"proper words in proper places." Brackenridge's own definition was "good sense expressed in clear language." To him, Bolingbroke and Shaftesbury often spoke "nonsense eloquently." He was fond of Sir Phillip Sidney's *Arcadia,* in which "there was ceremony without being ceremonious." If *Modern Chivalry* appears to ramble, it is by design. Brackenridge asserts that "good moral observations and anecdotes are the important elements—even when strung together as in Swift's 'Critical Dissertation on the Faculties of the Human Mind.'" The rambling structure of Montaigne's essays and Fielding's introductory chapters also charmed him. In spite of digressions in his own work, the loose organization guides the reader to the point, which usually is approached inductively and often ironically.

The burden of biblical and classical allusions borne in his early work lightened as his style matured in the West, and his sentences approached the simplicity of his model, Swift. His thought tended to move between sentences, rather than within them, as in the rigorously periodic prose of Samuel Johnson. Yet his sentences seldom move as lightly and comfortably as Addison's. A frequent raciness of diction, Brackenridge said in the Introduction to *Law Miscellanies,* gives "a certain flavor . . . that savours of the ancients." The tone of *Modern Chivalry* hardly ever resembles the polite bantering to be found in Addison. Achieving neither the starkness of Swift nor the relaxation of Addison, his style never satisfied him. Ruefully, he reflected near the end of *Modern Chivalry,* "*entre nous* . . . style is what I never could exactly hit. . . ."

In *Modern Chivalry* he alludes frequently to Lucian and Horace when he wishes to explain his satirical aims and methods. The only classical writer he claims as a direct model, however, is Xenophon, and the evidence is apparent. The Attic historian and friend of Socrates has usually been considered more of a journalist, a pamphleteer, and war correspondent than a scholarly historian or biographer, in spite of his *Memorabilia* on Socrates.

Brackenridge's allusions to the epic heroes of Homer and Virgil are never quite serious. One wonders if he does not see himself as a latter-day Homer who is perhaps a bit more obvious with his comedy. Brackenridge appears serious, however, in his references to the orators, Demosthenes and Cicero. The hortatory tones of his emulation ring everywhere in *Modern Chivalry*. It is the sense, however, not the sound, that guides these allusions. In addition to Demosthenes, Captain Farrago alludes to Solon and to the Pericles found in Thucydides, who indicate the sources of his political wisdom. Surprisingly, there are few allusions to Plato's Socrates. The quality of humble wisdom, which Brackenridge championed as the antidote to rich pride, had to be active in the body politic. To represent this quality, therefore, Brackenridge alludes not to Socrates but to Phocion, the Greek general who "came with plain coat from his humble dwelling and directed the counsels of people . . ." and to Cincinnatus, the Roman farmer-soldier who "was made dictator from the plough."

The thought in *Modern Chivalry* is outrageously redundant. All the dreamed utopias can become real in America if men seize their freedoms and employ them to seek knowledge and to refine their senses. Freedom itself is earned through cultivation of men's minds, just as the white man's rights to Indian soil are earned through its cultivation. Republicanism is the natural political form for a society of refined and free men; but a republic led by demagogues whom the ignorant elect is an abortion of the American dream. The fulfillment of the dream depends upon education, not upon the aristocratic concepts of the Federalists: "There is so much pride and arrogance with those who consider themselves the first in government, that it desires to be checked by the populace. . . ."

Until the mass of men become educated, the concepts of the Federalist party would most closely approach his philosophy. Then, as the French Revolution loomed, that party seemed to retreat from the American experiment and align itself with the monarchies. With the ideals of republicanism at stake, Brackenridge had to join its only defenders, the Jeffersonians. Even though their ignorant adherents on the frontier did mistake freedom for license, and desires for rights, he identified himself with these men. "For I am a democrat," he proclaimed in *Modern Chivalry*, "if having no cousin, and no funds, and only to rely on my personal services, can make me one."

Yet democracy was no visionary philosophy to Brackenridge. In his mind Thomas Paine was "an uncommon but uninformed man," and Rousseau and Godwin were examples of the "mere philosopher [who] is but a fool in matters of business . . . [and who] imagines nonsense." His experience with frontier politics served to reinforce rather than weaken the democratic ideal inspired by his classical education:

> I call myself a democrat. . . . I take my definition from a speech put into the mouth of Pericles, by Thycydides. It is to the Athenian people. "This our government is called democracy, because, in the administration, it hath respect, not to a few, but to the multitude: a democracy; wherein, though there be an equality amongst all men, in point of law, for their private controversies; yet in conferring of dignities one man is preferred before another to a public charge; and that, according to the reputation, not of his power, but of his virtue; and is not put back through poverty, or the obscurity of his person, as long as he can do service to the commonwealth."[17]

Practical and realistic, Brackenridge directed his criticism at the abuses of the democracy he found in action, so that respect for the multitude might assume genuine meaning rather than decay into the jargon of demagogues. He was thoroughly convinced that only a wise and virtuous electorate could long maintain self-rule. Such an electorate should be represented by either "a plain man of good sense, whether farmer, mechanic, or merchant; or a man of education and literary talents." If the satire in *Modern Chivalry* chastised the electorate, its realistic and reflective elements spoke to the individual man and revealed to him the "first springs of happiness in a republic."

CHAPTER 6

Incidents and Other Narratives

TODAY Brackenridge is recognized chiefly for *Modern Chivalry*. But, in his middle years on the frontier, he wrote two remarkable narratives that should prove of equal worth. They too foreshadow local-color qualities, but they deviate from all his other modes. "The Trial of Mamachtaga" and *The Incidents of the Insurrection* are not satirical; neither are they oratorical or reflective. Both are distinguished by an objective observation of scene, character, and action, and by a selection and an arrangement of these observations to produce climax. They are true accounts which bring to mind the fiction at the end of the nineteenth century that one calls realism.

Frontier life and the constant threat of Indian savagery were not fresh experiences to a man who had grown up in the Barrens. Consequently, even his first efforts at realistic writing, his communiques from the frontier, were something more than reportorial. They too had a purpose beyond mere communication. Development of a realistic art, in fact, can be traced from these crude exposés to the honed experience of *Incidents of the Insurrection*, a grossly mistitled narrative.

I Communiques from the Frontier

"The Narratives of the Perils and Sufferings of Dr. Knight and John Slover" describe the capture, the torture, the pleas and shrieks of the captives, and finally the escape of the two men who relate their stories. The narratives were sent to Freneau, who was then editor of *Freeman's Journal or North American Intelligencer*. *Freeman's Journal* carried the narratives in the issues of April 30, May 7, 14, and 28, 1783; and they were reprinted the same year in pamphlet form. In 1808 they were printed again with other Indian narratives Brackenridge had written in Archibald Loudon's *Selection of Some of the Most Interesting Narratives of Outrages, Committed by the Indians in Their Wars with the White People*. Brackenridge's "Narratives" are eyewitness accounts, "that of Slover taken by myself from his mouth as he related it"—accounts which represent the first communiqués from the frontier.

Their interest is chiefly historical (the writing is as raw as the subject); Brackenridge is concerned primarily in substantiating the accounts he has received. For example, he uses Slocum's narration as a check on Dr. Knight's: "It is well known that Mr. Slocum mentioned these circumstances at his first coming into Wheeling and before he could have known the relation of the doctor, for that this is an evidence of the truth of the doctor's account and his own." Brackenridge's concern with the exact dimension of things—"there stood a post about 16 feet in height . . . 3 piles of wood about 3 feet high"—is another effort at veracity, calling to mind the technique of Defoe. The reporter's own voice is heard only in a prefatory note which restates his beliefs that the Indians were savages who had no rights to a soil they did not cultivate and that treaties with them were useless.

Now, because Indians were barbaric in revenge, Brackenridge condemned them to extermination. These two captivity narratives, however, are his sole efforts at describing Indian savagery. In contrast, James Kirke Paulding dwelt on inhuman Indian tortures and remorseless rage in *Koningsmarke* (1836) and *The Dutchman's Fireside* (1831), both written after Cooper had popularized noble qualities in the American Indian. Paulding's cruel savages serve to illustrate Brackenridge's rhetorical "animals vulgarly called Indians" far more than those of Brackenridge. The Indians in Brackenridge's narratives are seen only through the points of view of the survivors. The purpose of the realistic detail, it should be remembered, is to shock the Easterners into action, into the commission of government troops for protection. As a result, the reader sees the details of atrocity, but instead of Indians he sees only blurs.

Unlike Paulding or Cooper, Brackenridge lived close to the Indians in the West, where it was essential to the life of the settlements to maintain an anti-Indian attitude. However, when he studied the individual Indian in "Trial of Mamachtaga," he saw neither a lofty son of nature nor a brute animal but a man unfit for Christian civilization because of his honesty as well as his depravity. Brackenridge does not bring the two views together. He rationalizes the necessity of taking Indian soil without consideration of the individual Indian, and he renders an Indian character in depth without relation to the total Indian problem.

II *"The Trial of Mamachtaga"*

"The Trial of Mamachtaga," written in 1785, tells of an Indian brought to justice for killing a white man. In spite of his loathing for the American Indian, Brackenridge was intrigued with this savage, whose name stood for trees blown in a tempest and who was rejected even by his own tribe. His intrigue allowed him to penetrate beyond predetermined notions of the American native as a noble savage or as a savage beast. A real portrait of the Indian character emerges, perhaps for the first time in American literature.

British writers had been emphasizing the noble-savage theme since 1688 when Mrs. Aphra Behn introduced it into her *Oroonoko.* In this treatment, the Indian symbolizes virtues that man might possess if freed of the debasing effects of civilization. Ruthlessness as an Indian trait was portrayed infrequently in England. In America the most common treatment before the nineteenth century was the narrative of captivity which reported actual experiences of white people abducted by Indians. Brackenridge's captivity narratives were preceded by many shocking "true relations," including the most vivid *Narrative of Captivity and Restauration* of Mrs. Mary Rowlandson (1682). In *The History of Maria Kettle* (1781), Mrs. Ann Eliza Bleeker relates a gruesome tale of a bloodthirsty attack by Indians who have lived peacefully with their victims until an opportune moment arises. When the father of the family goes on a trip, the Indians descend upon the family. This narrative renders the Indian as untrustworthy as well as cruel.

In Charles Brockden Brown's *Edgar Huntley* (1799) the hero thinks of Indians as utter beasts. Huntley, the sleepwalker, awakens in a cave to find his way out blocked by four brawny savages. His escape requires the killing of only one savage, but he cannot rest until he returns to slaughter the others. No sentiment or afterthought is stimulated by the killings. At no place in the novel does Brown indicate any disparity between his views and those of his hero, whose hatred was fixed by the murder of his parents at the hands of Indians.

However, some Americans of the eighteenth century offered sympathetic and ennobling views of the native. In the 1786 revision of "Rising Glory," Freneau cut out all passages referring to Indian savagery. In "The Dying Indian" (1784) and "The Indian Burying Ground" (1787) he regretted the passing of noble primitivity. In "The Indian Student" (1787) and "The Indian Convert" (1797) he showed how Christian education corrupted and degraded the natural nobility of the Indian character. Another favorable eighteenth-century view of Indians is found in Unca Eliza Winkfield's *The Female American* (1767), which presents a Captain Smith-Pocahontas kind of romance. At the end of this story the narrator, the offspring of the mixed marriage, rejects an offer to return to England, preferring a life with the noble savages whom she hopes to Christianize.

None of these eighteenth-century works actually combined the savage and noble qualities of the Indian. In *The Savages of America,* Professor Roy Harvey Pearce asserts that it was Cooper who finally set the pattern for other writers by treating the Indian as both noble and ignoble. One can substantiate this assertion by following the chronology of the Leatherstocking novels in which Indian nobility decays first in the tribes and finally in the individual, Chingachgook. Nobility is degraded by intruders who are motivated by mercantile interests, and the association of Leatherstocking with Indian virtues emphasizes Cooper's disdain of crass commercial classes. These attitudes are as antithetical to Brackenridge's concept of an enlightened populace as Cooper's self-reliant Leatherstocking and noble savages are antithetical to Brackenridge's ignorant frontiersman and vulgar animals known as Indians. Yet the attitudes of both writers converge to a single point; both see a future America run and ruined by a greedy commercial order.

But the conflict between the white man and the Indian who stood in his path was of no ethical concern to Brackenridge. Where Cooper regretted the degradation of Indian nobility,

Brackenridge regretted the lack of government forces on the frontier to protect the settlements from Indian raids. He focused always on the coming of civilization, not on the passing of wild life.

Actually, Brackenridge offered no philosophy about Indians as individuals. His arguments against Indian rights to the soil were political rationalizations. He saw the Indian as an individual only when his curiosity was aroused by events on the frontier, and then he wrote from observation which was rare, if not unique, in either late eighteenth- or early nineteenth-century treatment of Indians. In "The Trial of Mamachtaga" Brackenridge treats the Indian neither from an idealistic nor from a shocked point of view, but from a realistic one. Brackenridge tries to see the events as the Indian sees them. Consequently, the reader perceives in the respectable white men who try the Indian a fundamental lack of humane sentiment. They reveal themselves as utterly incapable of understanding the Indian or appreciating his culture.

Knowing that the frontiersmen will ostracize him, the narrator, Attorney Brackenridge, offers the defenseless Indian his services for a few beaver skins. The Indian's idea

> . . . was that he was giving the beaver as a commutation for his life. Under this impression it did not appear to me proper that I should take the beaver, knowing that I could do nothing for him; besides seeing the manner in which the dark and squalid creature was accommodated with but a shirt and breech clout on, humanity dictated that the beaver should be applied to procure him a blanket and food additional to the bread and water which he was allowed.

The attorney's interpreter, fearing his own skin, is reluctant to make the necessary purchases. Brackenridge is forced to buy the items himself, and through this act the narrator renders the town's mood. It is as savage as the prisoner is thought to be. When the townsmen discover that the interpreter is involved, they justify his fears by threatening to hang him. He saves his neck only by relinquishing all involvement with the case; but they almost hang him anyway, mistaking him for Mamachtaga on the day they decide to storm the garrison for a lynching party.

The pursuit of the interpreter provides comic relief in a somber mood.

At the trial, Mamachtaga displays a depth of honesty unknown to his white judges, whom he confuses with God and Jesus Christ. He cannot plead guilty because he does not know whether or not he killed. He was drunk at the time of the murder. Brackenridge misses no opportunity for humor, but he does not destroy the serious mood through exaggeration. He reports the humor as it occurs, without comment. Some humor is provided by the court officer in selecting the jury: "'Prisoner, look upon the Juror: Juror, look upon the prisoner at the bar. Are you related to the prisoner?' One of them, a German of a swarthy complexion and being the first called, took the question amiss, as thinking it a reflection and said with some anger that he thought that an uncivil way to treat Dutch people, as if he could be the brother or cousin of an Indian." The account of backwoods justice is also edged with humor; for example, there is the offhand manner in which the judge overrules testimony that white men had given the defendant whiskey. If true, Mamachtaga would not be held responsible for his crime. Without leaving the bar, the jury returns a verdict of guilty.

Asked why he should not be hanged, the Indian replies that he would rather "run awhile," the custom for the condemned in his tribe. The Indian's startling request is ignored. Ironically, as Mamachtaga awaits execution, he does get an opportunity to "run awhile." When the jailor's daughter becomes ill, he is asked to gather herbs for her in the woods. While he is at large, the only license he takes is to collect paints so that he may die the death of a warrior. Back in jail, a white prisoner awaiting execution asks that Mamachtaga do away with him, but the Indian replies that he has killed enough white men; and he reveals that he not only is resigned to his fate but sees the justice of it. As his body is released on the scaffold, the rope about his neck breaks; he falls to earth, alive. Climbing the scaffold a second time, he smiles, as though asking pardon for his clumsiness. He is hanged with this smile upon his lips. The author does not attempt to interpret the smile; but the story tells the reader that it too comes from the depth of his honesty, which is possible only in a creature fundamentally innocent of the white man's modes. The smile is not ironical for the Indian. He is ignorant of the virtue he has come to symbolize for Attorney Brackenridge and for the reader.

With the economy of modern short fiction, this little-known story produces a single effect and does so through an objective approach. The intended effect is never stated but is revealed through sharp selection of environmental details, actions, and characterizing elements; and the effect is wrought ironically from the point of view of a major character. Through Attorney Brackenridge, the reader recognizes in the savage some fundamental requirements for civilized individuals; and in the civilized white men, a fundamental savageness when acting en masse. The obvious lessons for democratic conduct are never obtrusive.

The story is rare for its time because the author ignored rather justifiable prejudices against the Indians and rather steadfast "morals" concerning the punishment of murderers. It compels sympathy for the Indian, though he is ugly by most ordinary standards. It investigates character, both of the social violator and of the society violated. In spirit as well as technique, "The Trial of Mamachtaga" fulfills the definition of realism given by Howells in *Criticism and Fiction:* "Realism is nothing more and nothing less than the truthful treatment of material. . . . We must ask ourselves before we ask anything else, Is it true—true to the motives, the impulses, the principles that shape the lives of actual men and women?" In this story Brackenridge does not shy away from penetration beyond the commonplace dear to Howells; yet he does not concentrate on the sordidness dear to some of the naturalists writing in the wake of Howells' realism.

"The Trial of Mamachtaga" was not published until 1808 after Brackenridge had returned east to Carlisle. Printed with another sympathetic study, *The Lone Indian*, in Archibald Loudon's collection, the two narratives offer a contrast to Brackenridge's early reports of Indian atrocities.

III Incidents of the Insurrection

Historical accounts of the Whiskey Rebellion usually emphasize the roles of Alexander Hamilton, who was Washington's Secretary of the Treasury, and Albert Gallatin, who was later Jefferson's Secretary of the Treasury. Hamilton, it seems, welcomed the uprising in Western Pennsylvania as an opportunity to demonstrate the strength of the Federal government and its right to enforce national laws within the states. The backwoodsmen grumbled about insufficient Federal protection against Indians, about navigation rights on the Mississippi, and about the loss of freedom under the new Constitution. They were ideal subjects for the demonstration. From Hamilton's own words, historians have inferred that his object in proposing the excise tax was to provoke resistance.

The moderate representative of Western resentment against the excise on whiskey was Albert Gallatin, a rich and respected gentleman who had taught at Harvard before moving West. He expressed himself in a constitutional manner. More violent opposition was instigated by a number of groups formed in imitation of the French Jacobin societies, among them the Mingo Creek Society which Brackenridge called "the cradle of the Insurrection." These societies encouraged bands of "whiskey boys" to raid stills that paid the tax and to mistreat tax collectors. The Rebellion itself started with the burning of the tax collector's house near Pittsburgh in 1794. One of the "whiskey boys" was killed in the gunfire exchanged with the militiamen who were defending the house. Succeeding events led to a rebel march on the Pittsburgh garrison. In this instance combat was averted largely through the influence of Brackenridge.

In *Incidents of the Insurrection,* Brackenridge rather than Gallatin had the leading role in moderating rebel tempers. It was certainly Brackenridge rather than Gallatin who earned the scorn of both sides after Washington called out fifteen thousand militiamen to quell the uprising which never really occurred. And it was Brackenridge who was held as an insurrectionist leader. Hamilton freed him after a prolonged hearing in which the cloud of suspicion was never quite dissipated.

Except for the praise of his journalistic enemy, William Cobbett (Peter Porcupine), and of his son, Henry Marie,[1] *The Incidents of the Insurrection in Western Pennsylvania in the Year 1794* has received no more consideration as literature than "The Trial of Mamachtaga."[2] Claude M. Newlin views it as historical data. Seeing the narrative as literature, the biographer makes only this comment:

In haste to put his account of his conduct before the people, he sent a packet of the manuscript to Philadelphia by each week's post. He did not even take time to correct the manuscript of his copyist, and, still worse, he forwarded some of the section in his own illegible handwriting. So the book was not only hastily composed, but . . . also badly printed. Nevertheless, the work was highly valued by at least one contemporary reader, William Cobbett, of no mean capacity for judgment.[3]

Since almost all other remarks pertaining to the narrative are historical, they ignore the psychological revelation of character under mob pressures and the evocative depiction of events, their causes, and the narrator's motives in guiding them. Instead, the comments invariably point to incriminating evidence of the author's guilt in the affair. For example, Daniel Agnew states in a sketch of Brackenridge: "The most doubtful part of Mr. Brackenridge's life was that during the Whiskey Insurrection of 1794 when he apparently sided with the Insurgents. That he was a delegate, met with the insurgents at Parkinson's Ferry and at Braddock's field, opposing the collection of the excise and seemingly approving of their proceeding, there can be no doubt."[4] And William Adel in *Bulwark of Liberty* agrees: ". . . he had fought the Federalists on the stump, in the press, and, it was suspected, by condoning, if not abetting the Whiskey Rebellion."

Some of these judgments may have stemmed from other accounts of the affair, such as the one in the diary left by a member of the Jersey troops sent to quell the insurgents: "It has been ludicrously observed in camp that the meaning of the parson was that the Jersey Blues will go on to Pittsburgh contrary to the pleasure of the Almighty and against the wish of the inhabitants of that place, which in a political sense is likened to Hell because Brackenridge, the worst devil of all the insurgents, resides there."[5]

Questions of Brackenridge's guilt fade, however, when the reader becomes absorbed in the literary effects of Brackenridge's narrative. Perhaps the digressions and intruding pleas of innocence have distracted readers from the psychological intensity as the narrator attempts to moderate the rebellious action that he cannot prevent. The tension increases throughout the lawyer's efforts at the risk of his life to outwit the mob by reasoned appeals to desires and egos. Perhaps the reader not anticipating literary experience overlooks the unfolding characterization of the insurrection leaders and the narrator's subtle manipulation of them. Most important, such a reader may fail to orient himself with the focal point of the book, the actions and reactions of the individual under the intense stress of social upheaval. He may also fail to appreciate the delicate treatment of the main character's internal conflict between his sympathies for the insurgents and his duties as a patriot. For want of editorial pruning, this dramatic and realistic narrative has been neglected.

Toward the end of his days, when disruption of the Union was again threatened, this time from the East, Brackenridge pointed to *Incidents of the Insurrection* as an example of the dangers being risked. He felt that his book provided ". . . a picture of a people broke loose from the restraints of government, and going *farther* than they had intended to go. If that book was republished at this time, and circulated in the Eastern States, it could not but contribute to shew the danger of even talking of a severance of the Union, or an opposition to the laws."[6]

The narrative is, precisely, a picture rather than an explanation or an apology, in spite of the author's first intentions; but it is far more than a picture of a people. It is the story of conflict between a torn people and a person who attempts to repair the rupture, and the story is presented with artistic awareness. Many of the events, re-arranged in time, are offered at the most pertinent point, as they impinge on the narrator's thought and action. The story opens in the lawyer's office where the United States Marshal seeks advice on serving writs to delinquent distillers and to persons who have attacked the tax collector. The lawyer's conflict between the law and sympathy for the cause of the insurgents is established immediately along with the tension of dealing with an aroused mob. The scenes of violence that have already occurred are rendered later, as the narrator is drawn deeper into the affair against his own desires.

The playfulness that disturbs the tonal unity in most of Brackenridge's work is completely avoided. He uses humor as a persuasive instrument. At the Mingo Creek meeting he arouses laughter when the members of the Jacobin society threaten violence. Aimed at diverting action, the humor is painfully pulled forth; and it enhances rather than disrupts the tone and the tension. His life is at stake at every meeting and in every mass action. And his position becomes more dangerous as the events proceed.

Brackenridge sympathetically portrays the leaders of both sides. Most of them seem to share his predicament of being drawn into the events reluctantly. David Bradford, a cowardly leader of the insurgents, is first seen at the height of his confidence and power. His bristling military manner repels the reader, but slowly the action reveals that he is posing; then the reader begins to pity him. Understanding that his conduct is treasonous, Bradford does not know how to avoid treason and still maintain his affluent position as an honorable man of the people. Brackenridge explains the motives of others in the Mingo Creek Society:

> Some of the leaders . . . had been disappointed in their wishes to be justices of the peace, or to sit upon the bench as associate justices; others were harassed with suits from justices and courts and wished a less expensive tribunal; others favored it as an engine of election for country offices, or for state legislation; others from a desire natural to men, of being conspicuous. This society was the cradle of the insurrection. They did not, as a society, project the first outrages, but they naturally sprung from the licentiousness of idea, with regard to law and liberty, which the articles of the institution held out or were calculated to produce.

Those unwilling to rebel against the government are also pressed into the cause, often ironically:

> . . . a breath in favor of the law was sufficient to ruin any man. It was considered as a badge of Toryism. A clergyman was not thought orthodox in the pulpit unless against the law; a physician was not capable of administering medicine unless his principles were right in this respect; a lawyer could have no practice without at least concealing his sentiments, if for the law. . . . On the contrary to talk against the law was the way to office and emolument. In order to be recommended to the government as a justice of the peace you must be against the law. . . . It was the shibboleth of safety and the ladder of ambition.

This statement, occurring in Volume III, summarizes the mood of the narrative; but it does so only after the author has rendered it through characters in action. In this atmosphere, the major character, Attorney Brackenridge, employs all his psychological insight to save his neck while persuading the inflammatory mob to forego the object of its enthusiasm—insurrection—and to adhere to his sense of right action—formal redress to the government. Any misstep or misstatement leads to violence and personal harm. The attorney equates his own destruction at the hands of the rebels with disruption of the Union, with civil war between East and West—a consequence that only he seems to comprehend fully.

Yet he is no hero. In personal conflicts involving government loyalty, community loyalty, and personal safety, he vacillates. Neither for nor against the insurgents, he appears to be one of them in Federalist eyes—and to be a Federalist in the eyes of the insurgents. When all nuance is put aside and the insurgents demand of him "whether we are to be supported . . . or left to ourselves," the attorney is forced to commit himself: "These were the words: they impressed me with an agony of mind." His own words, delicately selected, lead the insurgents to believe that he will act with them, but actually they tell only of his sympathy for their cause. Later at Braddock's Field the vacillation grows more apparent to the insurgents. Serving both sides, which are drawn up as if for battle, the attorney senses the change in the rebel view of him. Fearing his personal safety, he pretends a continued role in the negotiations; but he dwells only on means of escape from the scene, an escape he finally effects with the aid of a Federalist general.

The thrust of events amplify his vacillations between acting for his personal safety and for the social good. He contemplates emigration to the East: "I thought of being absent on some pretense that might be plausible; and it struck me to prevail with the people of Pittsburgh to appoint me as an envoy to the executive to state the motives of their conduct and explain their situation." And learning later that his efforts at conciliation have made him the symbol of insurrection in Eastern minds, he weighs the possibilities of waging war against the government:

Perhaps it [the insurrection] might claim these lands to the westward, and invite all the world to take possession of them. Collect all the banditti on the frontiers of the state, to help us fight for them; tell the Spaniards to come up to the mouth of the Ohio, and give us a free trade; let the British keep the posts, and furnish us with arms and ammunition; get the Indians of the woods to assist us; tell them that the people on the East of the mountains want our whiskey and their lands;—we might urge war, and perhaps succeed. It is true we should succeed to misery for awhile, and poverty at last. But even this would be more tolerable to me, than to live under circumstances suspected by the government, and treated with contumely by these people, when they had returned, loaded with the favors of the government, as having been the great defenders of it.

Finally, when the insurrection fizzles as the Jersey troops approach, the attorney fears that the officers will not restrain their men who have sworn violent oaths against his person. He meditates a run to the woods and a life among the savages; but, in a handbill to the troops, he had announced that he would stay. Awaiting arrest, he seeks solace in Plutarch's *Lives*. The philosophy of Solon tells him that citizens must take some role in a civil tumult or be put to death. He realizes that in the Athens of Solon, his efforts to moderate the social conflict would have been recognized, and he would not have deserved death; but on the frontier, far from the center of government, the role of moderator is not recognized. Here it is absurd to act according to Solon's law. The first law apparently is still self-preservation. Heroic concepts are for civilized minds, and he condemns himself only for his foolish adherence to such ideas.

When the troops arrive, he is spared death. His punishment is humiliation and social ostracism, both on the frontier and in the East. His humiliation is sharpened by the presence of his former college friend, General Henry Lee, who not only commands the troops but quarters himself in the Brackenridge home. Even after Hamilton clears him in a suspenseful sequence of hearings, the taint of treason adheres. Citizens mutter that he saved himself by turning state's evidence. He is a "most artful fellow." Walking the streets becomes a painful experience; he "contemplated the buildings a good deal." A social snub provides the warm domestic denouement:

A ball was now to be given. . . . Prothonotary Brison . . . declined sending the usual card to Mrs. Brackenridge. She was hurt; I saw the flush of indignation in her cheek, and sparkle of fire in her eye. I was offended for a moment. "What!" said I, "are you hurt at this? You insult me, because it is on my account you suffer the indignity. Did you not read to me the other evening, the life of Phocian?—after having rendered services to the state, and accused of treason by the arts of malignant individuals, and acquited by the people; suppose his adversaries to have taken their revenge by getting a master of ceremonies to exclude his wife from the ball; would you not think it more honorable to be the wife of Phocian, under these circumstances, than of a common Athenian, though you had received a card, and been called upon to lead the first dance . . .?" By this address to the pride of the human mind, I had a philosophress in a moment.

Nothing, however, soothes the pain churning his own breast: ". . . though I have not been arraigned at the bar of justice, yet from the first moment of obloquy against me, I have considered myself an arrested man. . . . From that day, the morning sun shone to me less bright; the light of night has been more obscure; the human countenance presented nothing but suspicion. The voice of the man hurt me; I almost hated life itself." The self-condemnation has passed with the terrible necessity that called it forth. He relies upon the example of Phocion's heroic conduct. Attorney Brackenridge survives his ordeal without any permanent impairment to his conscience. The impairment is social, not personal. The narrative lines of development lead to this interpretation, but the author's intention is openly to clear his name of suspicion. This intent is borne out by the insertion of testimonials, supporting documents, and other addenda in Volumes III and IV.

When the narrative elements are disassociated from the rest, they combine into a story of an idealistic yet ambitious man—a man caught in the complexities and dangers of social upheaval which lead him to a view of the base self beneath his ideals and ambitions, a view that is but a momentary glimpse. It passes with the dangers that unveil it. On a more obvious level, the narrative elements combine into a story of the individual's will exerted upon social forces in tumult. On the level of the author's overt intention, the narrative elements are but explanations of a man's conduct in the frontier turmoil known as the Whiskey Rebellion.

The insurrection was the major crisis in Brackenridge's life, and the account of it was a major turning point in his literary production. Cold reason could not exonerate him. His explanation had to appeal through emotions, through a total recreation of the intense situation in which he and the others had acted. The intensity is achieved through the selection of critical scenes that are rendered with sensuous description and inter- woven to sustain major threads of action, to develop characters bit by bit, and to reveal dominant themes. For example, there is the scene in which young Neville, the son of the tax collector, is introduced:

> At the moment we came to the river, we fell in with Neville, the younger, Marshall Lenox, and a young man of the name of John Ormsby of Pittsburgh, a family for whom I had regard; but knew the young man to be inconsiderate and rash; and was persuaded that on this occasion he acted without the knowl- edge, or at least the approbation of his parents: All these were armed, which I thought imprudent. I felt concern for them; and taking that liberty with the young man, which I could not take with others, I addressed him abruptly:—What! said I, Armed? Yes, said he. You will not ride with us armed. You may ride as you please, said he, I am armed. Neville, the younger, who was mounted on a gray horse, pistols in his holster, spoke:—we are not all born orators, said he: we are going to fight, you to speak. I thought him a better chevalier than a judge of the occasion.

The atmosphere established in this scene not only imparts reality but also suggests the epic. Neville's reply parallels the reply of Achilles in *The Iliad* after Agamemnon has told him, "you are gifted as a fighter." By characterizing the warriors through their history, prophesying impending disaster, and arranging oratorical contests of heroes, Brackenridge associates the significance of the present events with those of the glorious past. He is still working within the frame of the "Rising Glory of America."

The realism is psychological as well as scenic. On the eve of the march to Pittsburgh, for example, the narrator walks about the field of rendezvous and subtly attempts to instill fear, though he must be careful to appear in favor of the action: "Their [the insurrectionists] query everywhere was, were we to take the garrison? I answered always that we were. The query then was Could we take it? It was answered, No doubt about it. But at a great loss? Not at all; not above a thousand killed, and five hundred mortally wounded. This loss, to the more thinking part, appeared very serious."

Incidents of the Insurrection combines the characteristics of

Brackenridge's early and late writings. Under intense stress, the narrator calls upon his classical knowledge and thought habits to guide him. On occasion, he sees his material in terms of heroic similes: "when a scud of wind takes the standing corn of the farmer, and on the field bows the stalks to the earth, so languished my brother at the bar." And in the midst of terror he cannot resist the touch of satire: "Hearing that I had been considered as a leader of the insurgents, I thought I must endeavor to support the appearance, as I would be a good deal looked at." However, the light strains of satire never disturb the serious mood. They are matched with strains of sensibility, particularly in scenes portraying Mrs. Brackenridge and the insurrectionist Miller. As in *Modern Chivalry,* sentiment is again checked by an abiding realism. Sentimental portrayal of Miller's family, for example, emerges out of detailed observation:

> By this time, we had arrived at his house about eight miles from Pittsburgh. As we came up, three pretty children presented themselves in the inside of the fence that enclosed the cabin: and one of them said, putting his fingers between the rails, "Daddy, I have got a little brother."

> I was sensibly affected with the reflection that possibly that daddy might come to be hanged, and that brother fatherless before it could know that it ever had one. . . .

Brackenridge reports what he hears and sees, and how his mind reacts. For the first time, he renders frontier speech without satirical intent. Here Miller relates his grievance against General Neville, who had been appointed excise officer on the eve of the insurrection:

> I felt my blood boil at seeing General Neville along to pilot the sheriff to my very door. He had been against the excise law as much as anybody. When old Graham, the excise man, was catched and had his hair cut off, I heard General Neville himself say they ought to have cut off the ears of the old rascal: and when the distillers were sued some years ago for fines, he talked as much against it as anybody. But he wanted to keep in the Assembly then. But whenever he got an offer of the office himself, he took it. His mother and my mother were sisters. I was always for General Neville in his elections, and it put me mad to see him coming to ruin me.

Largely through his sensitive selection of language Brackenridge stimulates the reader's imagination so that he can create for himself what the story cannot realistically show. The tone, the attitude, the entire mental arrangement of the rebel leader, Tom the Tinker, is suggested through the author's presentation of this notice to the public:

> Poor Tom takes this opportunity to inform his friends throughout the country that he is obliged to take up his commission once more, though disagreeable to his inclination. I thought when I laid down my commission before that we had the country so well united that there would have been no more need for me in that line, but my friends see more need for me than ever. They chose a set of men whom they thought they could confide in but find themselves much mistaken, for the majority of them have proved traitors. Four or five big men from below has scared a great many, but few are killed yet. But I hope none of those are any that ever pretended to be a friend to poor Tom; so I would have all my friends keep up their spirits and stand to their integrity, their rights, and liberty, and you will find poor Tom be your friend. This is a fair warning; traitors take care, for my hammer is up and my ladle is hot. I cannot travel the country for nothing.
>
> From your old friend,
TOM the TINKER

Near the end of the narrative, Brackenridge declares a separate peace with society. He abandons the social responsibility that is dictated by his classical guide, Solon: "If the like scene should happen again, I will not conduct myself on the principle of Solon's law . . . let the executive and insurgents settle their own negotiations; I will have nothing to do with them."

CHAPTER 7

Miscellanies

THE WORK of Brackenridge is a fusion of literary forms and moods beginning in the eighteenth-century tradition of epics and mock heroics, then traveling the avenues of realism and reflection. More and more, as he reflected upon his life and work, a sensibility to native roots invaded his writings. Beginning with his Scottish poems, his writing assumed a wistfulness about his early idealism and his boyhood. His satirical powers waned or were eclipsed, and he sought solutions in the law for the problems of democratic society. The reflective mood dominates the introductions to his *Law Miscellanies* and *Gazette Publications*. It is also the mood of his "Epistle to Walter Scott," which pleads for a poet similar to Scott who can do justice to the beauty and spirit of the Western country. These, as well as extensive additions to *Modern Chivalry*, mostly expository and often reflective, comprise the major production in the last fifteen years of his life.

Although Brackenridge never reached the sentimental level of Bret Harte, the miscellaneous efforts of his late years are aimed at similar effects. In "The Argonauts of '49" Harte stated that his literary aim was to illustrate "an era replete with a certain Heroic Greek poetry, of which perhaps none were more unconscious than the heroes themselves." Looking through Brackenridge's late essays and poems, the reader can see this purpose resonating in all his life and work. With a public modesty also typical of Brackenridge, Harte added that he would be "content to have collected . . . merely the material for the Iliad that is yet to be written." This note sounds again and again in the reflections of Judge Brackenridge.

I Gazette Publications *and* Law Miscellanies

A major characteristic observed in Harte's work is the tendency, not to concentrate on the scene itself, but to look back
upon it. In this nostalgic mood Brackenridge collected his
Gazette Publications, material that would show in what "manner the human mind had employed itself in the past." The
human mind was his, and the collection did illustrate how exposure to frontier politics and embroilments had gradually led
him to abandon the epic approach to life and his grand manner
of portraying it. Except for the drama, *Battle of Bunkers-Hill,*
the collection consists of essays and poems written on the
frontier. It appears to contain all that Brackenridge could find
of them, and there is little evidence of a selective principle. The
major value lies in the early versions of materials that were re-
shaped in *Modern Chivalry,* such as the "Modern Chevalier,"
many Hudibrastics, and a still humorous "Memoir to the American Philosophical Society." The Scottish dialect poems are
refreshing surprises.

The introduction and conclusion evaluate his literary aims and
accomplishments. He considered himself a literary man, but he
referred to the collection as scraps for amusement. His primary
ambition, he said, had always been to write; but his was "not
an age or country that will make it the means of emolument, or
the way to honour." The opening and closing essays render the
feelings of a man of affairs who achieved some station in life
but at the expense of the dream he had set out to fulfill in
youth. Yet he did not regret his pursuits: ". . . though I would
rather be the poet than the Maecenas as to after-fame, yet it is
better to be the Maecenas as to present enjoyment. I would
warn therefore a son of mine against too much attention to some
parts of what may be called polite literature, as not fashionable in
our present state of society, and as a seducing syren from the
more profitable pursuits of life."

The major pursuit in the last decade of his life was an attempt
to refine the common law of Pennsylvania in a composition of
integrated chapters. The result was a disparate collection of reports appropriately entitled *Law Miscellanies.* He had intended
the volume to be a Pennsylvania Blackstone, showing how

Pennsylvania law differed from the English law; but, as he proceeded, he realized the extent of the undertaking and the limits of his knowledge. He settled for the collection of miscellaneous essays.

The collection illustrates more than anything else his sensing of defeat for his ideal of democracy and his consequent reliance on law to order the licentious mass that would not educate itself. Again he wrote against the current of his time. Since the attacks on the judiciary under the Jefferson administration, anything dealing with the law was tainted. Ironically, *Law Miscellanies* reveals Brackenridge's ingrained idealism and abiding romance of self. Idealism is apparent in his faith that the law could be unified, simplified, and clarified, and his romance in the belief that one man, Brackenridge, in the waning years of life, could accomplish such an enormous task. After claiming that Brackenridge was utterly ignorant of the law, Horace Binney praised the reports the author incorporated in *Law Miscellanies:* "a safer guide in practice, or a more respectable, not to say decisive authority in argument cannot be wanted by the profession."[1] David Paul Brown, another important legal mind of the time, found *Law Miscellanies* comparable to *Modern Chivalry* in "genius and humor."[2]

The essays criticize the unenlightened use of traditions and precedent, the feudal principles which still survived, and the tight naturalization laws. The Introduction to the *Law Miscellanies,* an essay on ethics and values, dwells on the need for grace of expression, on the problems of education—including finances—and on the languishing attitude of the youth in his time. Like the essay introducing *Gazette Publications,* the one in *Law Miscellanies* achieves more philosophical penetration than most of Brackenridge's other work because it was not written for an occasion or in the heat of political controversy. The style itself became more relaxed. Gone is the fire of the political sermons and orations; gone are the cadences, language, and the old devices of excessive symmetry and antithetical climax. The later essays are calm, the tone almost conversational; and the mood is of a man thinking, remembering, advising, and confessing. Absorbed primarily with the individual, they are retreats from social involvement:

It must be the result of every man's experience, that happiness consists in the employment of the mind upon some object, the attainment of which calls forth the energies of thought, or action. So that I consider the poet [Pope] as not going the whole length of the foundation of happiness, when he says,

> Reason's whole pleasure; all the jobs of sense,
> Lie in three words, health, peace, and competence.

For though without these, little pleasure can be enjoyed; yet, even with these, little can be enjoyed where there is wanting an occupancy of the mind.[3]

II *Scottish Poems*

A number of poems preserved in *Gazette Publications* illustrate a dimension of feeling unsuspected in the public life of Brackenridge. Two of them, written about 1790, are totally out of tone with the austere satire of the first volume of *Modern Chivalry* that he was composing at the time. One is an elegy occasioned by the death of his friend, the wife of Doctor Nathanial Bedford of Pittsburgh. From its opening stanza, the control of rhythm and sound is surprising:

> Whether the spirit doth survive
> The body and doth live
> In the Elysium of the Greeks
> Or heaven of which the Christian speaks,
> I know not; but, if there be
> Such immortality to thee or me,
> Fair shade, this thing call'd death
> And the mere stopping of breath,
> Not being to oblivion brought,
> Is a light matter in the scale of thought,
> And not the proper subject of a tear.

The treatment is not realistic, but sentiment is checked by the author's strong sense of Greek and Roman culture.[4] Ancient motifs of fate and fortitude, for example, are woven with those of sensibility—purity and innocence:

> For pure as Innocence and Love
> She felt the will of Jove,
> With proper forbearance complied
> And like the unstain'd lily dropp'd her head and died.

The other poem, "St. Andrew's Anniversary," is occasional, written for the Pittsburgh inhabitants of Scottish descent who, he tells us, "on the anniversary of St. Andrew (30th of November) were accustomed to celebrate his festival." The first of several pieces composed in Scottish dialect, this poem is another reaction, almost a recoil, from the embroilments of the frontier village. It is a nostalgic vehicle returning the poet to his roots where his limitations became most evident:

> For well I wat, the sangs aboon
> The lift are scarce as gude,
> And Scott's sauls even in the moon,
> Tae hear them wad rin wid.

> Wad pit them in the mind o' braes,
> And knows where they were born,
> And springs they play'd, and bony haes,
> They danc'd among the corn.

> Ah: had I but the soul o' sang,
> My kintra kens fu weel,
> The pleasant melody ere lang,
> Wad sound o'er vale and hill.

Similar strains of sensibility can be observed in "Trial of Mamachtaga," and may well have been expressed in unpublished poems now lost. (His habit was to stow his works in trunks, drawers, and other out-of-way places and then to forget them.) A developing sensibility, in fact, can be traced through the work of Brackenridge beginning with "Cave of Vanhest," printed in the first seven issues of *The United States Magazine*.

Six years after "St. Andrew's Anniversary," Brackenridge again employed the Scottish dialect to compose a series of poems in response to those of David Bruce, who ran a country store near Pittsburgh. These poems stem from a base of real experience. Unlike the clumsy Hudibrastics, they reflect through the senses rather than the intellect; and, unlike his early fiction and other poetry, they pull at experience stored in the subconscious. His own youth and the Scottish folkways replace the abstraction of beautiful life experienced in dreams, and affection for his past tends to replace social criticism. The sensibility is combined with a humor which has deepened through the suffering endured in the Whiskey Rebellion. This humor, which emerges in various scenes of *Incidents,* dominates the Scottish poems. The Scots-Irishman, as Bruce called himself, was willing to pay the excise for a blessing so precious as whiskey:

> Then foul befa' the ungratefu' diel
> That wou'd begrudge to pay right well
> For a' the blessings that ye yiel
>   In sic a store;
> I'd nae turn upo' my heel
>   For saxpence more.[5]

Brackenridge could not abide the "sixpence more," but the native sound of this poetry overwhelmed him. Calling himself Aqua Vitae, Brackenridge joined Bruce in praise of whiskey and agreed that law and order were necessary. His prime interest was not in explaining his own position; it was in the verse that flowed from a man of his own blood:

> For where's the man that now-a-day
>   can sing like Burns;
> Whom nature taught her ain strathspeys
>   and now she mourns.[6]

The nostalgia deepens in the second series five years later, after Brackenridge had been appointed to the Supreme Court and was attempting a reconciliation between contending parties on the frontier. In a single issue of *Tree of Liberty* (June 20, 1801), he printed a humorous appeal to peace, "On the Means of Reconciling Parties," and then continued his poetic exchange with David Bruce. In the opening poem he compares a boyhood experience in the Barrens—an attraction to a small rabbit that turns out to be a skunk—with his relations to the Scots-Irishman:

> To think at last, out owre these woods,
> Amang the simmer trees and buds,
> A bardie should spring up, a musie,
> A genuine Parnassus pousie,
> In nature real, and in mew,
> Of Arcady a *Kitlin'* true.
>   My wishes led me to caress it
>
>   .   .   .   .

> I thought me o' what happen'd early,
> When *Skunkie* pish'd upon me fairly
> When I had ta'en it for a rabbit,
> And did na think it would grow crabbit.
> Sae frae the verra self same things,
> Our guid and evil aften springs;

And then he appeals once more for conciliation:

> But still the consolation's ta'en
> Hard words, and language break nae bane.
> While I can laugh and take a drink,
> I'll be to them that evil think.
> Here's to the bardie; fill the cogue; . . .

Near the end of the series the Brackenridge poems become mere responses to the accusations of the Scots-Irishman. The defense of his drinking, for example, becomes almost as shallow and thudding as his Hudibrastics:

> It may be true; but there is BURNS
> Wha gars us laugh and greet by turns,
> Wad tak a drink; alack! o'er muckle;
> But wha o'er gie'd him o'er the knuckle,
> For that which made the bard so canty,
> And gied us a' his sangs sae dainty.[7]

There is little satire in these poems. The humor is warmed by wistful reflections upon the sights, sounds, and activities of the Scotsmen on the frontier, and by reminiscence of earlier traditions. They sound none of the gay, celebrative notes of Burns. They comprise no effort to establish a revival of Scottish folk poetry on this side of the Atlantic as the songs of Burns had done in his homeland. Although Brackenridge owned a collection of Scottish poetry and songs, as did Burns, he was out of the milieu and could not immerse his senses in the actual sounds of the vernacular as Burns could. Brackenridge's Scottish verse, therefore, would lack the naturalness and spontaneity of Burns, even if Brackenridge had possessed equal musical genius. Where Burns could directly represent, Brackenridge could only reminisce. For example, one may compare Burns's "To a Mouse" (1786):

Wee, sleekit, cowrin, tim'rous beastie,
Oh, what a panic's in thy breastie!
Thou need na start awa saw hasty,
    Wi' bickering brattle!
I wad be laith to rin an' chase thee,
    Wi' murdering pattle!

with Brackenridge's treatment of an animal:

As ance a thing just leke a cat,
I saw, and what wa'd I be at,
But try to grip it, a wild pousie
And bring it home to catch a mousie,

Before I knew what I was doing,
Or mischief that the thing was brewing,
A spout o' water frae its tail
Came on me; O the smell, the smell.

Burns focused all attention on the mouse at the present moment; Brackenridge focused on himself, on his own remembered sensations.

Under the influence of Burns, who died the year Brackenridge began the Scottish poems to Bruce (1796), the verse took a natural turn. Rhythm, sound, and sense coalesce. Although he did not achieve the lyrical qualities of Burns, his language was no longer fettered by mock-heroic mechanisms. Like those of his countryman, these Scottish verses are autobiographical and concerned with rural domesticity. The satire is slight; he aims no hard blows at specific objects. In place of conscious efforts to achieve the eloquence of classical and Augustine poets, the tendency is lyrical, expressing less wisdom derived from life than the experience of life itself.

III Modern Chivalry, *Part Two*

Whatever is good about the second part of *Modern Chivalry* owes its value to the happy concurrence of the material with the author's pervading mood: it is good whenever the material contains the stuff of sensibility. Brackenridge knew his satirical powers had evaporated; indeed, he lamented this fact in later pages and also admitted the loss of desire to outfit his strictures with appropriate dress. Unfortunately, he found no unifying device to substitute for the narrative of the first part of *Modern Chivalry*. Even more unfortunate, he did not recognize the literary legitimacy of his mood. Consequently, he was enticed by his mood into the kind of reflections found in the Scottish poetry and then, forcibly disciplining himself, turned about and continued his endlessly redundant lessons to grown-ups.

The epigraph from Juvenal's *Satires* that appears on the title page of *Modern Chivalry—Quicquid Agunt Homines, Nostri, Farrago Libelli—*would best introduce Part Two. It translates: "Whatever men do, wishes, fears, anger, pleasures, joys, and different pursuits, of these is the hodgepodge of our book." (In his habitual haste, Brackenridge relied on memory and missed some of the original quotation.) *Farrago* means *hodgepodge*. The slight and erratic narrative of Part Two may have been the author's intention for the entire work, and it may have been overwhelmed by his invention of Teague who immediately took over the author's imagination in his brash way and pushed Farrago to the side, much as Falstaff must have pressured Prince Hal aside in Shakespeare's imagination. The Captain, however, has retaken command in Part Two; this section is mostly a collection of ideas, fancies, and criticisms of American democracy and other relevant and irrelevant matters that stuck in the author's mind from 1801 to 1815.

The impulse of Part Two is to retaliate in satire for the outrages the author had suffered at the hands of the "blackguard press" as head of the Jefferson party in Western Pennsylvania. Following events, however, Brackenridge switched after the first few chapters to a defense of the law which Jefferson's party seemed to threaten after it came to power. In the opening chapters, therefore, Teague has become an editor; soon after, he obtains a seat on the bench where Brackenridge then ignores him. The satire quickly dissipates in Farrago's didacticism.

Without Teague, the Western mob becomes the Captain's direct foil. No longer does he anticipate a public facility for reasoning. Thus, instead of imparting his wisdom in appeals for correct conduct, he shrewdly manipulates; he exercises rather than dispenses his wisdom. Also, the wisdom itself has changed. His classical education is discernible, but it guides his thought only so far as it corresponds to his recent lessons on the frontier.

Humor, born in reflection, frequently interrupts the author's arguments. As in the Scottish verse, it warms the discourse:

> The principal and professors had harangued in vain. It was threatened that if they did not stand out of the way, they would burn them with the college.

> The Captain had come up and ventured to speak. "Gentlemen," said he, "it is not for the college that I am about to speak; it is for yourselves. Your object is to put down learning; and do you not know that it is put down already? Why will you do a useless thing? It is calling in question your understanding to do a needless mischief. . . . Take a horse jockey, and in two weeks from the jump he is in a pulpit. No need of Latin, Greek, Hebrew, a polyglot bible, systems of divinity, a commentary, a treatise, an essay or a dissertation. All is plain sailing now. All this tends to put learning down so that you have all the advantages of this without the trouble. Why burn the college? The building will serve useful purposes when the professors are driven out of it.[8]

Here and there in Part Two the philosophical weight is lightened by nostalgic descriptions of Western life. They are delightful oases touched by the author's sense of realism. Some of these contain his most effective writing, as in this description of a settler taking a wife:

> A cattle-driver had come from the western settlements to exchange at the fair stock for salt, iron, and women. In barter for the last article, a cow was given for a girl. The settler went out in the first instance with a rifle, a hatchet, and a knapsack. Having fixed on a spot at a spring head, the next thing was to fall saplings and construct a hut. A small piece of ground was then cleared of the underwood and this formed into a brush fence to enclose it. He returned then to the interior of the country; and the next summer, going out with a hoe and a stock of provisions on a pack horse, he began his cultivation. Having tamed a buffalo or got a cow from Padan Aram, he had in due time milk in abundance. This put it into his head to get a milkmaid, in other words a wife. The traders in this article usually chose those of the less opulant, whose dress answered all the ends of fashion without the affectation. The elbows were bare because the sleeves did not reach, the folding doors of the bosom were undrawn because they had been always open. There was no occasion for flesh-colored pantaloons, for the pantaloons were the

natural flesh itself, discovered through the rents of the muslin by the waving of the wind, like a light cloud upon a bed of air in an April day.[9]

Writing in the comparative calm of Carlisle, removed in distance and time from the scenes of violence, Brackenridge could even reflect with good humor upon his enemies of the Whiskey Rebellion. Looking back, he sensed the mythical qualities of Tom the Tinker's whiskey boys, which moved him to try a literary form alien to his cultivated mind—the ballad. The "Song of Clonmel," appearing suddenly among the author's more leaden reflections, is a complete and most pleasant surprise. Clonmel is a fictional ballad singer associated with the whiskey boys who, after the insurrection, have taken to the woods where they live in their own "madcap settlement." In spite of the anapestic doggerel, Clonmel's reflections must have enlightened the author's reclining years:

> What use is in fighting, and gouging, and biting,
>   Far better to let it alone;
> For kicking and cuffing, and boxing, and buffing,
>   It makes the flesh ache, and the bone.
> But give me the whiskey, it makes one so frisky,
>   But beating, and bruising makes sore;
> Come shake hands, my cronies, come near, my dear honies,
>   And think of your grudges no more.
>
> .   .   .   .
>
> There is nothing like love, which comes from above,
>   And tickles the youngsters below.
> It is vain man's own fault, that he so brews his malt,
>   As ever to cry out, heigh-ho!
> Alexander and Caesar, and Nebuchadnezzar,
>   Found out to their cost this was true;
> Now who will be fools, to drink at the pools,
>   Of ambition, and war, we or you?[10]

Disappointment in his literary career is nowhere evident in Part Two of *Modern Chivalry.* It reveals contrarily the highest confidence in his literary worth:

. . . were all the books in the world lost, this alone would preserve a germ of every art. . . . Yet disliking egotism and all appearances of vanity in others, I am unwilling to emblazon beyond what is moderate, a production of my own. But to speak my mind a little freely, leaving the bible out of the question . . . and conceding to Homer his superiority; and to Shakespeare and Plutarch's Lives, I do not know but I certainly flatter myself that my performance may occupy the next grade.[11]

In 1815, at the end of the final volume, he boasted that five printers had already made fortunes out of his novel and that in Pennsylvania there existed "scarcely a parlor window without *Modern Chivalry.*"

IV *"Epistle to Walter Scott"*

Before leaving the frontier to assume his judicial duties at Carlisle, Brackenridge started a correspondence with Jefferson that inspired him to attempt a poem eulogizing the future president in the grand style of his idealistic days at Princeton. The leaden verses of "Jefferson: In Imitation of Virgil's Pollio" are an effort to show the fulfillment of the hopes in "Rising Glory":

The Western earth rejoices at the event,
By flood and field and the whole heavens extent,
As giving philosophy the government.
Columbia views it, and is pleased the while;
And you her son will recognize the smile.

Apparently the frontier could not dissipate Brackenridge's classical training. In spite of his satirical turn, real poetry for Brackenridge existed only in the sober line from Virgil through Milton. In *Gazette Publications* he regrets having lived at a time when the pursuit of poetic excellence was not possible. Perhaps the environment of his times was also responsible for his prosaic personality. He failed to recognize the need for a nimble imagination in the making of a poem, and he may have confused imagination with the fancy required for his satirical efforts. To write a serious poem one needed rather the knowledge of serious poetry and an excellent mind. Classically, there was a definite way to do it; models existed. The principle of selectivity applied to selection of the proper model for the proper writing situation. It was a logical act.

Reading Scott's "Lady of the Lake" on a visit to Pittsburgh in 1810, Brackenridge was moved once again to emulation. This time his purpose was to compose a similar pastoral that would render the beauty of the Western country and all it had meant to him. Unlike his previous efforts in the grand manner, the material that he wished to use in this poem had been experienced deeply. He learned at last that poetic imagination merely tantalized him, that it existed beyond the reach of his mind. Abandoning his own pastoral effort, he rendered his ineptitude in an "Epistle to Walter Scott." Clumsily he imitated his countryman's octosyllabics and pointed up his own crude verse as the living demonstration of his failure. The ineptness of his verses, of their awkward rhymes and stumbling rhythms, and of their inappropriate allusions to classical names reinforce the sense of the poem in much the same way Pope's adept verses reinforce the sense of his "Essay on Criticism." The classicist in Brackenridge could not quite let go of Homer and Virgil, even as he cried out amateurishly: "Oh give me Burns, oh give me Scott; I want no more when these I've got." Burns and Scott become true descendants of the classic poets, and thus Brackenridge joins the attitudes of eighteenth- and nineteenth-century literature.

The mood in Brackenridge's "Epistle" is regret that the beautiful American wilderness has no Scott to immortalize it; and, though he will try, he has not the genius:

> Here by Ohio's stream my pen
> Gives image to a sort of strain
> Which feeling prompts but Genius none,
> So gifted to a native son.
> My gift is only to admire;
> In madness I attempt the lyre,
> At hearing this celestial sound
> From Scotia's hills and distant bound
> Of this I dream and when awake,
> I read the Lady of the Lake.

A poetic experience emerges from the very clumsiness of the non-poet who desperately seeks to fulfill the poetic need. The impulse is to mirror nature for individual pleasure and exaltation,

not social utility, the only purpose his society seems to recognize
in living:

> Inglorious I must bend my head,
> And think of something else than fame,
> Though in my bosom burns the flame
> That in a happier age and clime
> Might have attempted lofty ryme.

To the end Brackenridge clung to the "Rising Glory."

CHAPTER 8

America Lies Beyond

ALTHOUGH Brackenridge's open attacks on backwoods ignorance won little public favor for himself or his ideas, he was esteemed as a man of eloquence in his own day and for decades after it. Apparently, he had a reputation for eloquence as early as 1779, when the President of the United States, members of Congress, and the Minister of France were invited to hear his "Eulogium of the Brave Men Who Have Fallen in the Contest with Great Britain." His *Modern Chivalry* was read over the frontier, back East, and at least by the French king in Europe. In June, 1839, the editor of the *Pittsburgh Literary Examiner and Western Monthly Review* wrote, "Twenty years ago this work [*Modern Chivalry*] . . . was the humorous textbook of all classes of society."

And, according to Professor Quinn in *American Fiction*, the originality and vigor of the book "carried it into great popularity, especially in the West, where his name became a household word for half a century." Henry Marie Brackenridge was surprised to find the book had penetrated to the remote settlement of New Madrid, Missouri, by 1810: "From your name, sir," the village justice inquired of him, "may I ask whether you are related to the author of *Modern Chivalry?*" Learning that his visitor was the son, the justice exclaimed in awe and admiration, "What! . . . the son of the author of *Modern Chivalry!*"[1] Henry Marie's letter to Philip Egalité informs us of the king's attention: "I have read that your Majesty sometimes speaks of the author of *Modern Chivalry*—will your Majesty be pleased to accept a copy of that work as a token of remembrance from his son?"[2] Editions of *Modern Chivalry* in 1825 (Wilmington); 1846, 1856 (Philadelphia); and 1926 and 1937 (New York) indicate its continuing interest in the East. After reading it in Boston, John Quincy Adams was sufficiently impressed to seek the descendants of Brackenridge years later on a visit to Pittsburgh.[3]

Literary historians generally acknowledge Brackenridge as the author of the third American novel, after William Hill Brown's *The Power of Sympathy* (1789) and Susanna Rowson's *Charlotte Temple* (London, 1791). When his work is represented in anthologies, it is always with a chapter or two from *Modern Chivalry*.[4] Unfortunately, his achievement in satirizing early American politics, institutions, customs, and character has overshadowed the remainder of his work. Professor Parrington acknowledges that he "tried his hand at various kinds of polite literature, producing a masque, a poetic drama on Bunker Hill, prose essays, some sermons, and turned at last to satire"; but he regards *Modern Chivalry* as the "single noteworthy contribution to American letters by Hugh Henry Brackenridge."[5]

Parrington explains the general confusion resulting when *Modern Chivalry* is judged as the author's sole effort: "*Modern Chivalry* has proved somewhat of a puzzle to later critics who have not cleared their minds of the old cobwebs of Federalist criticism. Thus a literary historian, William G. Cairne, has suggested that it is a 'half-hidden satire on democracy,' and he inclines to number it among the literary ram's horns that were blown against the walls of the democratic Jericho."[6] Percy H. Boynton recognizes the significance of the novel but dismisses it with the pert statement that it is "a jumbled thesaurus of Americana."[7]

The writings of Brackenridge span the last years of colonial America, the Revolution, and the incubation of democracy on the frontier. The portrait he drew of the early American frontier is the most significant portion of his work; no similar literature exists for this period. This portrait is given its fullest significance in the stream of events, thoughts, and moods that flow out of the author's Eastern works. Because literary historians cannot accommodate the complete work of minor writers in their task of organizing the nation's literature, the stature of Brackenridge remains obscure. Historians must work with literary norms which help render, with proper emphasis, the total body of our heritage, as Wellek and Warren explain in *Theory of Literature:*

> It should be frankly realized that a period is not an ideal type or an abstract pattern or a series of class concepts, but a time section, dominated by a whole system of norms, which no work of art will ever realize in its entirety. The history of a period will consist in tracing of the changes from one system of norms to another. While a period is thus a section of time to which some sort of unity is ascribed, it is obvious that this unity can be only relative. It merely means that during this period a certain scheme of norms has been realized most fully. . . . Thus the survival of a preceding scheme of norms and the anticipations of a following scheme are inevitable, as a period is historical only if every event is considered as a result of the whole preceding past and if its effects can be traced into the whole future.[8]

I *The Literary Frontier*

In 1928, the American Literature Group of the Modern Language Association identified the literary norms in a collective effort, *Reinterpretation of American Literature.* Several essays in this collection found a key to the American character in the following statement by Professor Frederick Jackson Turner: "The advance of the frontier has meant a steady move away from the influence of Europe, a steady growth of independence in American lives. And to study this advance, the men who grew up under these conditions, and the political, economic, and social results of it, is to study the real American part of our history."[9]

In the first essay, Pattee calls "the first generation of the republic, 1790-1830, enormously important" and points to its literature—the early novels "curiously enough produced in Boston" and the "amazing sensations of the *Sketch Book* and Cooper's *Spy.*" The second generation, the era of Andrew Jackson, is the period of tumultuous democracy: "It was not until 1829 that the East was really awakened by their war whoop."[10] Brackenridge, clearly out of place in either generation, was writing on the frontier when the literary focus was still in the East; and he had died by the time the focus changed to the West.

The essay by Norman Foerster does not fix the frontier spirit in time but finds this "key to the definition of Americanism . . . strangely neglected" in American literary history.[11] He agrees with Turner that the frontier is "the most American thing in all America. . . . As generation followed generation, the frontier in North America shifted westward, ever renewing itself and ever sending back to the east currents of thought and feeling and power that in large measure determined the development of American democracy."[12] But, according to the essay by Professor Jay B. Hubbell, the frontier has been a legend rather than a reality: "Although much of our political history was made on or near the frontier, our books have as a rule been written by authors, and for readers, quite remote from the frontier. American literature is necessarily a paler, less distinct reflection of the frontier than is our history. . . . Many aspects of frontier life vanished before being accurately described."[13] It appears that the detailed portrait of frontier life and thought found in the works of Brackenridge should be most significant; and this apparent importance grows more concrete in the essay by Howard Mumford Jones, who asserts that historians of American literature write

> . . . as if the New England divines must of necessity have been followed by the political literature of the 18th Century, and this in turn by the Hartford wits, the Knickerbocker group, and what not, until Transcendentalism and Poe and the realistic novel and contemporary poetry arrive in due course . . . [this] is not progress, it is a series of amazing jerks. . . . No period of our letters is more unsatisfactorily organized than the stretch between the publication of the *Federalist* and the emergence of New England Transcendentalism. I think this has been true because the principle of its organization has not been grasped. It was the period of the conservative reaction.[14]

Professor Jones, while calling for a new approach to the period, is also thinking only in terms of the East. The conservative reaction must refer to Washington and Hamilton and to revulsion against the French Revolution. He is not thinking of the frontier, of Jeffersonian democracy, and of the attitudes favoring the French Revolution. In any new approach to the literature of the period, according to Professor Jones's suggestions, the apparent significance of Brackenridge would fade.

Not until modern American historians discuss the second quarter of the nineteenth century do they concentrate on the frontier spirit. Consequently, Brackenridge is aligned with the literary norm of his time—with the revolutionary period rather than the frontier—and his significance is generally equated with that of *Modern Chivalry,* an early novel somewhat more valuable than its sentimental predecessors, *The Power of Sympathy* and *Charlotte Temple.* The most characteristic appraisal was given by Lillie Loshe in 1907: "The satirical form of didacticism, which gave rise to the large family of eighteenth-century Quixotes, is represented in America by Hugh Henry Brackenridge's *Modern Chivalry.* . . . [Brackenridge] displays more ability than any American story teller before Charles B. Brown. . . . At his best, Brackenridge shows great satiric power, and a vigorous clearness of style unusual in that day of somewhat tawdry elegance in fiction."[15]

Seldom is *Modern Chivalry* associated with succeeding movements in American literary history. Although Parrington does not relate *Modern Chivalry* to later literature, he does relate it to Jacksonian democracy. In *The Colonial Mind 1770-1800,* he finds the novel presents "the rough and tumble democracy in action" and its author is "a realist concerned with realities." To Parrington, its mood is "redolent of stump lands and their rude leveling ways. . . . The preposterous spectacle of a pushing fellow with no qualifications setting himself up for high office was to become more frequent with the later rise of Jacksonian democracy."[16] One notes, however, that Parrington's title, *The Colonial Mind,* for the first volume of *Main Currents in American Thought,* implies that the novel belongs in the colonial period rather than in the succeeding period which he calls *The Romantic Revolution in America,* his second volume.

Ironically, Henry Adams' *History of the United States,* not burdened with the task of organizing our literature, is able to express the relationship directly: "*Modern Chivalry* was not only none too refined for its subjects, but more thoroughly American than any book yet published or to be published until the letters of Major Jack Downing and the *Georgia Scenes* [by A. B. Longstreet] of forty years later."[17]

II *Neglected Valleys*

Rarely is the other work of Brackenridge discussed in literary histories or included in anthologies. When it is, his writings of the Revolutionary period receive the attention. His patriotic dramas written for school production in Maryland have received perhaps more attention than they merit in Moses Coit Tyler's *Literary History of the American Revolution:*

> It is in spite of their literary defects [those of early American drama]—their crudity, dullness, coarseness, provincialism—that they are worth the moment's glance. . . . [They] are frank witnesses to the throes of mental and moral anguish through which we had to pass in order to become a nation. But we now approach two examples of dramatic writing having a literary merit so positive and so remarkable as to justify our study of them even on that account alone . . . the *Battle of Bunkers Hill* and the *Death of General Montgomery*. . . . [They contain] scene after scene . . . [of] tenderness and nobility.[18]

And Arthur Hobson Quinn writes in the *History of the American Drama:* "The verse of Brackenridge is flexible and dignified. . . . Brackenridge's dramas are better than the other revolutionary plays from the point of structure and expression even if they have not the vigor of action. . . . It is interesting that he chose defeats for his celebration but they were defeats that were greater than victories for they revealed the triumph of characters."[19]

The United States Magazine has also received notice. Frank Luther Mott states it is "probably the most brilliant performance of the whole period."[20] Pattee claimed it as "a most notable landmark in American literary history. Its methods as we view them today seem singularly modern and its materials and arrangements are indeed remarkable . . . against the background of their times. [It is] a spirited, intensely patriotic and highly literary periodical."[21]

Occasional references to the poor quality of Brackenridge's Hudibrastics tend to divert any further interest in Brackenridge as a poet.[22] "Rising Glory" is generally discussed as Freneau's poem with a parenthetical acknowledgment of Brackenridge. The *Literary History of the United States* describes the poem as "the personal dedication of a young poet steeped in the lore of his calling. Freneau would be a poet and he would sing a clear new song."[23] Unfortunately, the part of the poem quoted was written by Brackenridge.[24]

His Scottish dialect poetry, his "Epistle to Walter Scott," and his "Burial of Mrs. Bedford" are ignored.[25] His *Incidents of the Insurrection* has received no critical attention since Peter Porcupine found that "His perspicuity, his simplicity, his picturesque minuteness conduct his reader into the scene of action. You see, hear, and feel, just as the author actually did, and this itself is a talent of high excellence."[26] Porcupine's description implies realism, which is clearly out of phase with literary norms in the year 1795.

The contributions of Brackenridge to political thought also appear to be out of phase. In *American Idealism*, Floyd Stovall seems to set the stage for an introduction of Brackenridge: "The real America is . . . not to be found either in the order of the long settled communities or in the disorder of the frontier, but in that area of dynamic and expanding life which is born out of the union of the two. . . . This union of West and East, of the frontier spirit with the intellectual heritage of the past, was exemplified in the mind and character" not of Brackenridge, as one would anticipate, but of Thomas Jefferson. Stovall continues most significantly: ". . . It is doubtful whether [Jefferson's] ideals could become a force in world affairs, however, if they had not been caught up by the expansive enthusiasm of the frontier and carried, with the American flag, across the continent."[27]

On the frontier of Western Pennsylvania, it was Brackenridge who "caught up" the ideals, who founded and led the Jeffersonian party, and who established the *Tree of Liberty* to spread his political thought among the frontiersmen. Almost alone he attempted to join the frontier spirit with the intellectual heritage of the past. Nevertheless, *American Idealism* contains no reference to Brackenridge or to his work; nor do most histories devoted specifically to the literature of the frontier.

In *Beginnings of Literary Culture in the Ohio Valley*, W. H. Venable mentions the fact that Brackenridge contributed to the *Pittsburgh Gazette*, but he ignores all work except *Modern Chivalry*, which he describes through quotations from Duyckinck's *Cyclopaedia of American Literature* as "a century-old piece of Scotch wit and wisdom." In a less specific treatment of frontier literature, Ralph Leslie Rusk's *The Literature of the Middle Border* (1925), Brackenridge is excluded from the literature of the Ohio Valley. Lucy Lockwood Hazard's *The Frontier in*

American Literature (1941) treats "The Puritan Frontier," "The Southern Frontier," "The Hunter and Trapper," "The Golden Age of Transcendentalism," "The Frontier of '49," "The Golden Age of Industrial Pioneering," and so on. The chapter called "Hunter and Trapper" accounts for the period of early westward movement, and its literature is represented by Cooper and Irving. Brackenridge is not mentioned.

Realizing the possible significance of "neglected valleys between the better known peaks of our literary history," the American literature group that had produced *Reinterpretation* in 1928 published a series of essays in 1953 called *Transitions in American Literary History*.[28] The problem was not to evaluate the literary norms identified in the earlier work but to find "How and especially why American literature did change historically from one center of emphasis to another." The period between "dominant puritanism and formal romanticism," labeled earlier as "frontier spirit," was described as "the most complex . . . in American intellectual and literary history."[29] All the complexities, however, are confined to contradictions in the writers of the East. In Leon Howard's essay concerned with this period, Brackenridge is relegated to footnotes, but his work is a steady source of reference for the necessary discussion of attitudes towards the American Indian: "To the readers of newspapers he [the Indian] sometimes appears as no more than a dirty drunken beggar—as a one-eyed tawny character known as 'Blind Sam' did when he wandered out of his local gutter and had a considerable social success in a Pennsylvania city where the 'noble savage' had become fashionable."[30]

In spite of Brackenridge's abundant evidence to the contrary, Howard's essay presents the noble view of the Indian as the inclusive American view:

. . . thoughtful and observant Americans . . . collected evidence. And from their evidence rather than from romantic dreams, they drew their picture of the Indian who was, according to the researches of Jefferson, eloquent in council, courageous in battle, and affectionate in his devotion to his family—whose constitution, according to the observations of the trader James Adair, breathed liberty and equality—and whose achievements, according to the poet [Joel] Barlow and the historian Samuel Williams, included the establishment of a monarchy more happy and benevolent than any before recorded in history of unchristianized mankind . . . a savage almost as noble as any developed in the European literary tradition.[31]

Whether Brackenridge's contradictory view of "animals vulgarly called Indians" should also be considered as representative of a large part of American opinion of his era is less significant than the assumption that the "empirical quality . . . was so widespread that it was becoming a characteristic element in American literature."[32] If this assumption is true, it cannot be based upon the evidence presented; for the observers mentioned in the essay resided in the East with the exception of James Adair, an Indian trader and by necessity a friend to Indians.

This essay in *Transitions* not only follows the common practice of attributing "Rising Glory" to Freneau with a passing reference for Brackenridge, but also assigns exclusively to Freneau "Father Bombo's Pilgrimage,"[33] even though Pattee wrote some fifty years earlier that "The part signed H. B. is unquestionably the best; the prose is vigorous and the movement rapid. The only merit in Freneau's section lies in its lyric lament at the close of one of the chapters."[34]

Transitions elevates Brackenridge to a position above the footnotes in an effort to explain "The Decline of Neo-Classicism," an essay by M. F. Heiser covering the period 1801 to 1848:

Roughly speaking, the chronological configuration of new classical thought and expression in America may be indicated by three overlapping circles. . . . The second circle, the central one, is neo-classical in form and thought. It encompasses Franklin and Paine, much of Freneau and Barlow, Brackenridge, Rush, the deists, Jefferson and early Unitarians, including *immigrés* like Priestley and Thomas Cooper. A typical figure is H. H. Brackenridge whose *Modern Chivalry* written in installments between 1792 and 1815 is the most complete (800 pages) expression of the neo-classical spirit in the new nation.[35]

Although *Modern Chivalry*, a picaresque work, has the characteristics of eighteenth-century satire, it can hardly be said to typify "the neo-classical spirit." In the words of Brackenridge, it was written for "Tom, Dick and Harry in the Woods"; and the language and material tend to carry out the author's intention. In "The Decline of Neo-Classicism," the work is also seen as a "detailed picture of the beginnings of self-seeking individualism and leveling to the masses which were to supersede the conservative idea of social solidarity in nineteenth-century America." But the essay does not associate this work with the literature of the West; and this omission serves to obliterate the robust, realistic portrait of the early American frontier shaped through the other works of Brackenridge. A concluding statement in "The Decline of Neo-Classicism" implies the reasons for omission: "The west and the American Indian before 1830 were generally treated with urbane satire." Missing is the phrase, "treated from the Eastern point of view."

Generally, the *total task* of literary historians justifies their treatment of Brackenridge. Perhaps *Transitions in American Literary History,* devoted to the significance of work in the "valleys" of literary movements, must also adhere to the "peaks." It is apparent that neither the peaks nor the valleys that lie west of the Alleghenies come into historical focus until a decade after the death of Brackenridge.

III *Significance*

In mood, thought, and manner most American literature produced before 1800 resembles the products of England; and perhaps that is why Emerson and others would not recognize it as American. Actually American literature had been growing more distinctive as writers turned away from the East. Perhaps the first discernible break with English modes was the practical prose of Benjamin Franklin. The agrarian spirit forced another break. One perceives it early in Woolman's *Journal,* and later the spirit matured into the sedate political writings of Jefferson. Thomas Paine introduced a plain language that appealed to the uneducated and established a new prose tone. Philip Freneau's love of his own land propelled him out of the English mock-heroics and into a poetry that quite early sang the American dream. Anthologies permit Americans to see that all these breaks with the English literary modes parallel the movements of history—the political rupture with England and the founding of the new nation.

At least one distinctive break with English literature, however, does not parallel the drawn lines of our history. One literary man of the eighteenth century—a trained classicist—ventured West in the last days of the Revolutionary War. His work reflects the mood and thought of the American frontier decades before attention is focused on movements West and on the literary attitudes summarized as romanticism. Brackenridge's best work, completed before 1800, is clearly out of phase with the usual view of America's literary development. His narratives, short fiction, poetry, and essays fuse into a portrait of new country far from English dominance. At the center of the portrait is the antipathy of the frontiersman to Eastern influences and propositions such as the new Federal Constitution. By showing democracy at work in the new land, Brackenridge not only brings into focus the disunity of national ideals, but he also renders the image of an American cultural pioneer planting seeds of education, art, communication, and a sense of political idealism on the frontier; and of suffering personal defeat in return.

When the literary spotlight finally turned west, it shone upon a farther West, one beyond the early American frontier. Rendering the incubation of the American spirit as it was evolving out of English tradition and into Jacksonian democracy, the work of Brackenridge represents a most vital transition in American literary history. Perhaps the meaning of this transition is stated most cogently in Emerson's often quoted assessment: "Europe extends to the Alleghenies, America lies beyond."

Notes and References

Chapter One

1. Madison Papers, XIII, p. 9; cited by Fred L. Pattee (ed.), *Poems of Philip Freneau,* I (Princeton, 1902), xxi.

2. Fred L. Pattee, "Introduction," *Poems of Philip Freneau,* I, ciii.

3. *United States Magazine* (Philadelphia, 1779), p. 483.

4. These events are described in Sarah H. Killikelly, *The History of Pittsburgh* (Pittsburgh, 1906), p. 270; Claude M. Newlin, *The Life and Writings of Hugh Henry Brackenridge* (Princeton, 1932), pp. 59-111; and Leland D. Baldwin, *Pittsburgh: The Story of a City* (Pittsburgh, 1938), pp. 111-14.

5. "It is Tom, Dick and Harry in the woods that I want to read my book. I do not care though the delegated authorities never see it." *Modern Chivalry,* ed. Claude M. Newlin (New York, 1937), p. 471. All references, unless otherwise noted, are to this edition.

6. "On the Popularity of ———," *Pittsburgh Gazette,* December 1, 1787. His first use of the term *Hudibrastic* appears in the satire "On the running away of the nineteen members of assembly from the house, when it was proposed to call a convention to consider the new system of congressional government: and on the apology made by them in their address. A Hudibrastic," *Pittsburgh Gazette,* November 3 and 10, 1787.

7. *Modern Chivalry,* pp. 76-77.

8. Vernon Louis Parrington, *Main Currents in American Thought* (New York, 1927), I, 131.

9. Robert E. Spiller, *et al.* (eds.), *Literary History of the United States* (New York, 1948), I, 180.

Chapter Two

1. *Modern Chivalry,* p. 758.

2. Carl Holliday, *Wit and Humor of Colonial Days* (Philadelphia, 1912), p. 273.

3. *Tree of Liberty* (Pittsburgh), June 20, 1801.

4. Henry Marie Brackenridge, "Biographical Notice of H. H. Brackenridge, Late of the Supreme Court of Pennsylvania," *Southern Literary Messenger,* VIII (January, 1842), 2. Other quotations from

Hugh Henry's son appearing in these paragraphs are from the same source.

5. John Witherspoon, "Lectures on Moral Philosophy," *Works*, III (Philadelphia, 1802), 419.

6. Pattee, *op. cit.*, I, xix.

7. Newlin, *Life and Writings*, p. 15.

8. *Modern Chivalry*, p. 167.

9. Quoted from Pattee, *op. cit.*, I, xxii-xxiii.

10. *Modern Chivalry*, p. 455.

11. Claude C. Robin, *New Travels Through North America*, trans. Philip Freneau (Boston, 1784), p. 17.

12. Address to the troops at Morristown, New Jersey, *Gazette Publications* (Carlisle, 1806), p. 265.

13. *The United States Magazine*, p. 43. Leon Howard finds these octosyllabics a thorough imitation of Milton's "L'Allegro," citing, for example, "Maids of Virgin-Beauty Fair," and "widows gay and debonnair," which are among the more successful lines. ("The Influence of Milton on Colonial American Poetry," *The Huntington Library Bulletin*, No. 9 [April, 1936], p. 74.)

14. *Gazette Publications*, p. 227.

15. *The United States Magazine*, pp. 483-84.

Chapter Three

1. *Pittsburgh Gazette*, June 21, 1798.

2. *Gazette Publications*, p. 7.

3. "To the Inhabitants of Westmoreland County," *Pittsburgh Gazette*, April 28, 1787.

4. *Law Miscellanies* (Philadelphia, 1814), p. 512.

5. *Gazette Publications*, p. 39.

6. His marriage is assumed since his son was born the following year. Brackenridge does not mention his first wife anywhere. In the Introduction to his 1937 edition of *Modern Chivalry*, p. xiv, Claude M. Newlin states: "By 1785 he had definitely settled down in Pittsburgh. He had purchased land, built a house, and contracted a marriage with a Miss Montgomery."

7. *Gazette Publications*, pp. 23-24.

8. *Pittsburgh Gazette*, September 2, 1786.

9. "To the Electors of Westmoreland County," *Pittsburgh Gazette*, September 9, 1786.

10. *Pittsburgh Gazette*, January 20, 1787.

11. *Ibid.*, February 10, 1787.

12. *Ibid.*, January 6, 1787. For fuller accounts of this incident,

see Alston G. Field, "The Press in Western Pennsylvania to 1812," *Western Pennsylvania Historical Magazine* (December, 1937), XX, 231-64; and George T. Fleming, "Early Social Life in Pittsburgh," *Gazette Times*, February 15, 1920.

13. *Incidents of the Insurrection* (Philadelphia, 1795), III, 13.

14. *Gazette Publications*, p. 76.

15. *Pittsburgh Gazette*, March 22, 1788.

16. *Incidents of Insurrection*, III, 6-8.

17. *Ibid.*, III, 13-14.

18. Henry Marie Brackenridge, *Recollections of Persons and Places in the West*, (Philadelphia, 1834), p. 10.

19. *Gazette Publications*, p. 90.

20. John Pope, *A Tour through the Southern and Western Territories of the United States* (Richmond, 1792), p. 14.

21. *Ibid.*, pp. 15-16.

22. *Incidents of the Insurrection*, II, 14.

23. "Thoughts on the Excise Law," *National Gazette*, February 9, 1792.

24. *Pittsburgh Gazette*, July 6, 1793; *National Gazette*, July 27, 1793.

25. *A Political Miscellany* (New York, 1793), pp. 27-31.

26. "Biographical Notice," p. 5.

27. *Recollections of Persons and Places in the West*, p. 42.

28. *Ibid.*, p. 70.

29. *Pittsburgh Gazette*, August 16, 1800.

30. *Ibid.*, December 21, 1799.

31. *Ibid.*, August 23, 1800.

32. David Bruce, *Poems Chiefly in the Scottish Dialect* (Pittsburgh, 1801), p. 100.

33. *Tree of Liberty*, July 25, 1801.

34. *Ibid.*, September 13, 1800.

35. *Ibid.*, September 20, 1800.

36. *Ibid.*, January 31, 1801.

37. *Writings of Jefferson*, ed. H. A. Washington (Washington, 1853-54), VII, 451.

38. *Recollections of Persons and Places in the West*, p. 112.

39. C. C. Binney, *Life of Horace Binney* (Philadelphia, 1903), p. 40.

40. David Paul Brown, *The Forum, or Forty Years Full Practice at the Philadelphia Bar* (Philadelphia, 1856), I, 400.

41. *Modern Chivalry*, pp. 280-81.

42. *Recollections of Persons and Places in the West*, pp. 53-54.

43. "Biographical Notice," p. 19.

44. *Pittsburgh Record,* November-December, 1933. Cited by Agnes Lynch Starrett, *Through One Hundred and Fifty Years: The University of Pittsburgh* (Pittsburgh, 1937), pp. 496-97.

45. William W. Edel, *Bulwark of Liberty* (Carlisle, Pa., 1950), p. 124.

Chapter Four

1. For comparison, see Fred L. Pattee, *Poems of Philip Freneau* I, 49-84.

2. *Ibid.*

3. Preface, "Poem on Divine Revelation" (Philadelphia, 1774). For a critical comparison showing Brackenridge's poetic indebtedness to Milton, see Thomas P. Haviland, "Hugh Henry Brackenridge and Milton's 'Piedmontese' Sonnet," *Notes and Queries,* CLXXVI (April 8, 1939), 243-44; and "The Miltonic Quality of Brackenridge's Poem on Divine Revelation," *PMLA,* LVI (June, 1941), 588-92. And also Leon Howard, "The Influence of Milton on Colonial American Poetry," *The Huntington Library Bulletin,* No. 9 (April, 1936), pp. 63-89.

4. Thomas Paine, *Works,* ed. M. D. Conway (New York, 1894), I, 167.

5. "Poem on Divine Revelation," p. 14. Thomas D. Haviland, in "The Miltonic Quality of Brackenridge's 'Poem on the Divine Revelation,'" pp. 558-92, points out the "large and heavy debt" to Milton's phraseology. Examples:

> The Rosy hours brought on its beauty mild
> The day-spring from on high and from the top
> Of some fair Mount Chaldean, shephard's view
> That Orient star which Beor's son beheld

> From Aram east, and mark'd its lucid ray,
> Shedding sweet influences on Judah's land
> (p. 6 of "Divine Revelation")

Twice in *Paradise Lost,* Milton used "day-spring" and on several occasions, "orient," and "lucid"; "The orient wave" in "Nativity Ode," "orient liquor" in *Comus,* "lucid stream," and "lucid arms" in *Paradise Lost.*

> No more of Lybian Jove, Dodona's oaks
> In sacred grove give prophecy no more.
> Th' internal dieties retire abash'd
> Our God himself, on earth begins his reign:
> (p. 10, "Divine Revelation")

Compare with Stanza XXV of "Nativity Ode":

Nor all the God's beside
Longer dare abide . . .
Our Babe to shew his Godhead true,
Can in his swadling bands controul the damned crew

And finally,
. . . these happier shores
Where birds of calm delight to play . . .
(p. 14, "Divine Revelation")

Compare with "Nativity Ode," lines 66-68.

. . . the milde ocean
Who now hath quite forgot to rave,
While Birds of Calm sit brooding on the charmed wave.

6. *The Death of General Montgomery* (Philadelphia, 1777), Act V, Scene 5, note.

7. Newlin, *Life and Writings*, p. 35; Thomas P. Haviland, "Hugh Henry Brackenridge and Milton's 'Piedmontese' Sonnet," cited in Note 3.

8. Moses Coit Tyler, *Literary History of the American Revolution* (New York, 1897), II, 210.

9. Arthur Hobson Quinn, *A History of the American Drama from the Beginning to the Civil War* (New York, 1923), p. 53.

10. *Six Political Discourses founded on the Scripture* (Lancaster, 1778), p. 12.

11. *Ibid.*

12. "Before the Battle of Brandywine," *Gazette Publications*, p. 132.

13. *Political Discourses*, p. 60.

14. *Ibid.*, p. 7.

15. Holliday, *op. cit.*, p. 276.

16. *Political Discourses*, p. 11.

17. Preface, *The United States Magazine*.

18. *The United States Magazine*, p. 196.

19. *Ibid.*, p. 163.

20. Frank Luther Mott, *History of American Magazines* (New York, 1930), I, 27.

21. *Pennsylvania Gazette*, November 1, 1740.

22. *American Magazine*, January, 1741, p. viii.

Chapter Five

1. "Gloom of the Tory Satirists," *Eighteenth Century English Literature*, ed. James L. Clifford (New York, 1950), p. 11.
2. Dryden's Dedication to his translation of *Satires of Juvenal*.
3. "On the Popularity of ————," *Pittsburgh Gazette*, December 1, 1787.
4. "The Modern Chevalier," *Gazette Publications*, pp. 311-12.
5. *Modern Chivalry* (Philadelphia, 1815), IV, Appendix, I.
6. *Pittsburgh Gazette*, December 1, 1787.
7. *Modern Chivalry*, p. 805.
8. *Ibid.*, p. 3.
9. Published by John Scull on the presses of the *Pittsburgh Gazette*. The February 9, 1793, issue of the paper advertised:

> Modern Chivalry
> Volume III
> By H. H. Brackenridge
> Just published and to be sold by the Printer
> Price—Three Shillings and Nine Pence.
> Pittsburgh, February 23, 1793
>
> N.B. A few copies of the first and second
> Volume may be had in this town.

10. *Literary Examiner and Western Monthly Review*, I (June, 1839), 195.
11. Newlin, *op. cit.*, p. 306. See also laudatory comments in Parrington, I, 390-93.
12. Quinn in *American Fiction*, (New York, 1937), pp. 9-11. For a fuller analysis of local-color characteristics, see Roger Walterhouse, *Bret Harte, Joaquin Miller, and The Western Local Color Story: A Study in the Origins of Popular Fiction* (Chicago, 1936). In *American Local Color Stories* (New York, 1941), p. x, Harry R. Warfel and G. Harrison Orian find that the term local color "dominated a surface realism delighting in oddity, whimsicality, idiosyncracy, and in those stubborn, inbred character traits which lend themselves to comic treatment or caricature." Although these characteristics appear abundantly in Brackenridge's satirical work, these editors of local-color stories do not find them in American literature until 1832 in James Hall's *Legends of the West* (p. xvi). In *The Local Colorists* (New York, 1960), pp. 1-3, Claude M. Simpson derives the characteristics of local color from Hamlin Garland's *Crumbling*

Idols (1894). Its major distinction is emphasis on "differentiae, not on the generic." And its characteristics are literal description of local setting, authentic representation of real language of men in a locale, and picturesque treatment of oddities. Generally, according to Simpson, local-color materials were departures from commonplace norms. They were "cultured islands" or past ages of local individuality (p. 15).

13. Ernest Jackson Hall, *The Satirical Element in the American Novel* (Philadelphia, 1922), p. 81.

14. Newlin, *op. cit.*, p. 307.

15. Tremaine McDowell, "Sensibility in the Eighteenth-Century American Novel," *Studies in Philology*, XXIV (June, 1927), 399.

16. *Ibid.*, p. 396. In "A Reading of 'Wieland,'" *PMLA*, LXXVII (March, 1962), 51-57, Larzer Ziff maintains that Charles Brockden Brown turns against the sentimental tradition, "revealing its hollowness even as he exploited it." The evidence Ziff presents is Clara's overcoming of her maidenly reserve when she goes to Pleyel's house to assure him that she has not been faithless and finds that she cannot break through the barrier of Pleyel's sentimental conventions. He will not listen. The article, however, does not account for the fact that Clara and Pleyel do make up in the end, complying with the sentimental convention.

17. *Modern Chivalry*, pp. 530-31.

Chapter Six

1. William Cobbett, *Porcupine's Works*, I (London, 1801), 312; and Henry Marie Brackenridge, "Biographical Notice," p. 18.

2. Aside from Newlin's references in *Life and Writings*, the only apparent notice of the story appears in a historical article which employs it as evidence; see J. W. F. White, "The Judiciary of Allegheny County," *Pennsylvania Magazine*, VII (1883), 148.

3. Newlin, p. 176.

4. Daniel Agnew, *Sketches of Prominent Lawyers of the Allegheny County Bar of the Last Century and Earlier Years of This* (Philadelphia, 1889), p. 8.

5. From the diary of Quartermaster John Higg Clumm, quoted from "The Library," *Pennsylvania Magazine*, LXXI (1947), 56-57. Accounts of the insurrection were also written by Henry Marie Brackenridge, *History of the Western Insurrection in Western Pennsylvania, commonly called the Whiskey Insurrection* (Pittsburgh, 1859); Neville B. Craig, *Exposure of the Many Misstatements in H. M. Brackenridge's History of the Whiskey Insurrection* (Pittsburgh,

1859); and William Findley, *History of the Insurrection in the Four Western Counties of Pennsylvania* (Philadelphia, 1796).

    6. *Modern Chivalry*, pp. 765-66.

Chapter Seven

    1. Horace Binney, *Reports of Cases Adjudged in the Supreme Court of Pennsylvania* (Philadelphia, 1809-1815), III, 625.

    2. Brown, *op. cit.*, I, 396.

    3. Introduction to *Law Miscellanies*, p. 1.

    4. According to Gilbert Highet in *The Classical Tradition*, p. 292, the new literature of sensibility was a "spiritual and, therefore, more lasting rebirth of the Greek and Roman culture . . . in the soul of Western man."

    5. Bruce, *op. cit.*, p. 12.

    6. *Gazette Publications*, p. 240.

    7. *Tree of Liberty*, February 14, 1801.

    8. *Modern Chivalry* Part II, Volume I, Book I, Chapter 8.

    9. *Modern Chivalry* Part II, Volume I, Book II, Chapter 8.

    10. *Modern Chivalry* Part II, Volume I, Book III (Observations following Chapter 10).

    11. *Modern Chivalry*, p. 727.

Chapter Eight

    1. Henry Marie Brackenridge, *Recollections of Persons and Places in the West*, p. 188.

    2. Ms. copy of letter in 1846 edition of *Modern Chivalry*; cited by Newlin, *op. cit.*, p. 197.

    3. William McCandless, *Ex-President John Quincy Adams in Pittsburgh in 1843* (Pittsburgh, 1873). Judge McCandless quotes Adams' letter: "I had read the first part of *Modern Chivalry* and formed a pleasant acquaintance with Captain Farrago and his man Teague at their first appearance, more than half a century ago, and they had then excited much of my attention, as illustrations of life and manners peculiar to the times, and localities not entirely effaced, when I became more familiarly acquainted with them by this visit. . . . I shall read it over again, I have no doubt, with a refreshing revival of the pleasures with which I greeted it on its first appearance." Cited by Newlin, pp. 190-91.

    4. Selections from *Modern Chivalry* appeared in ten out of twenty-seven single and multiple-volume anthologies surveyed by Ben Fuson: *Which Text Shall I Choose for American Literature?* (Parkville, Missouri, 1952), Table III.

5. Parrington, *op. cit.*, I, 390.

6. *Ibid.* Parrington is quoting from William B. Cairn's *History of American Literature* (New York, 1930), p. 127.

7. Percy H. Boynton, *Literature and American Life* (Boston, New York, 1936), p. 136.

8. Austin Warren and René Wellek, *Theory of Literature* (New York, 1949), p. 278.

9. Frederick Jackson Turner, *The Frontier in American History* (New York, 1920); cited by Jay B. Hubbell, "The Frontier," in *Reinterpretation of American Literature* (New York, 1928), p. 39.

10. Fred L. Pattee, "A Call for a Literary Historian," in *Reinterpretation*, pp. 18-19.

11. Norman Foerster, "Factors in American Literary History," in *Reinterpretation*, p. 28.

12. *Ibid.*, p. 29.

13. Hubbell, "The Frontier," in *Reinterpretation*, p. 43.

14. Jones, "The European Background," in *Reinterpretation*, p. 70.

15. Lillie D. Loshe, *The Early American Novel* (New York, 1907), pp. 22-23. See also John R. Hendrickson, *The Influence of Don Quixote on Modern Chivalry* (unpublished dissertation, Florida State University, 1959).

16. Parrington, *op. cit.*, I, 390.

17. Henry Adams, *History of the United States of America* (New York, 1889-1901), I, 124-25.

18. Tyler, *op. cit.*, II, 210. Tyler also considered Brackenridge's political sermons as important American literature of the Revolution. See p. 297.

19. Quinn, *History of the American Drama from the Beginning to the Civil War*, p. 53.

20. Mott, *op. cit.*, I, 27. The most extensive treatment of the *United States Magazine* is given by L. N. Richardson's specialized *History of Early American Magazines, 1740-1789* (New York, 1931), pp. 196-210.

21. Pattee, "Introduction," *Poems of Philip Freneau*, I, xxix.

22. See, for example, *The Cambridge History of American Literature*, I, 287.

23. Spiller, *op. cit.*, I, 170.

24. The quoted lines were excluded when Freneau published his part separately. In the first edition of his poems (1786), Freneau explained: "This poem is a little altered from the original (published in Philadelphia in 1772), such parts being only inserted here as were written by the author of this volume." Cited by Pattee, *Poems of Philip Freneau*, I, 49. See also p. 78, which shows that the lines quoted in *Literary History of the United States* were actually written

by Brackenridge. Another mistake allowed by the editors of this work is contained in the following passage: "For years a judge in Pennsylvania, he knew at first hand the rough politics of democracy, yet his point of view in *Modern Chivalry* is generally that of an objective observer," p. 179. Brackenridge became a judge in 1799, some six years after the first volumes of *Modern Chivalry* were published and two years after Part I had been completed.

25. One critic has discussed Brackenridge's early poetry in relation to Milton: see T. D. Naviland, "H. H. B. and Milton's 'Piedmontese' Sonnet," *Notes and Queries,* 176 (April 18, 1939), 243-44, and "The Miltonic Quality of Brackenridge's *Poem on Divine Revelation,*" *PMLA,* LVI (June, 1941), 588-92. Lewis Leary discussed "Father Bombo's Pilgrimage to Mecca" mostly with reference to Freneau, in "Father Bombo's Pilgrimage," *Pennsylvania Magazine of History and Biography,* LXVI (October, 1942), 459-78.

26. Cobbett, *op. cit.,* I, 312.

27. Floyd Stovall, *American Idealism* (Norman, Oklahoma, 1943), pp. 20-21.

28. Harry Hayden Clark (ed.), *Transitions in American Literary History* (Durham, North Carolina, 1953), p. x.

29. Leon Howard, "The Late Eighteenth Century," *Transitions,* p. 51.

30. *Ibid.,* p. 77. The note for this passage refers to Brackenridge's *Gazette Publications.*

31. *Ibid.,* pp. 78-79.

32. *Ibid.*

33. *Ibid.,* p. 85.

34. Pattee, "Introduction," *Poems of Philip Freneau,* I, xix.

35. M. F. Heiser, "The Decline of Neo-Classicism, 1801-1848," *Transitions,* p, 96.

Selected Bibliography

PRIMARY SOURCES

Satires against the Tories. Written in the last War between the Whigs and Cliosophians in which the former obtained a compleat Victory, with Philip Freneau and James Madison. Ms. Am0336, Historical Society of Pennsylvania, c. 1770.

Father Bombo's Pilgrimage to Mecca in Arabia. Vol. II, Where in is given a true account of the innumerable and surprizing adventures which befell him in the course of that long and tedious Journey. Till he once more returned safe to his native land, as related by his own mouth. Written by H. B. and P. F. 1770, with Philip Freneau. Ms. Am0336, Historical Society of Pennsylvania.

The Rising Glory of America, with Philip Freneau. Philadelphia: R. Aitken, 1772.

A Poem on Divine Revelation. Philadelphia: R. Aitken, 1774.

The Battle of Bunkers-Hill. Philadelphia: Robert Bell, 1774.

The Death of General Montgomery, at the Siege of Quebec. Philadelphia: Robert Bell; Norwich: J. Trumbull; Providence, 1777.

Six Political Discourses Founded on the Scriptures. Lancaster: Francis Bailey, 1778.

The United States Magazine: A Repository of History, Politics, and Literature Vol. I, ed. Philadelphia, 1779.

"The Cave of Vanhest," *United States Magazine* (1779).

"On Enfranchisement of the Negro," *United States Magazine* (1779).

"An Eulogium of the Brave Men Who Have Fallen in the Contest with Great Britain," *United States Magazine* (1779); also Philadelphia: F. Bailey, 1779.

"The Establishment of the United States," *United States Magazine* (1779).

"Dissertation on Indian Rights to the Soil," *United States Magazine* (1779).

"Narrative of a Late Expedition Against the Indians, with an Account of the Barbarous Execution of Col. Crawford and the Wonderful Escape of Dr. Knight and John Slover from Captivity in 1782," *Freeman's Journal, or North American Intelligencer* (April 30, May 7, 14, 28, 1783); also Philadelphia: F. Bailey, 1783.

"An Account of Pittsburgh," *Pittsburgh Gazette* (July 29, 1786).

"An Answer to a Challenge," *Pittsburgh Gazette* (August 19, 1786).

"Observations on the Country at the Head of the Ohio River, with Digression on Various Objects," *Pittsburgh Gazette* (August 19 and September 2, 1786).

"To the Electors of Westmoreland County," *Pittsburgh Gazette* (September 9, 1786).

Letter by "Angus MacMore," *Pittsburgh Gazette* (December 30, 1786).

Letter from Philadelphia, December 16, 1786, reporting activities in State Assembly, *Pittsburgh Gazette* (January 6, 1787).

Letter defending county vote in the Assembly, *Pittsburgh Gazette* (March 17, 1787).

An answer to criticisms by William Findley, *Pittsburgh Gazette* (March 24, 1787).

"To the Inhabitants of the Western Country," *Pittsburgh Gazette* (April 21, 28, May 5, 12, 26, June 2, 9, 1787).

"A Masque, Written at the Warm-Springs in Virginia in the Year 1784," *Pittsburgh Gazette* (June 16, 1787).

Defense of vote in the Assembly on the Pittsburgh church bill, *Pittsburgh Gazette* (June 23, 1787).

A Letter to the Rev. S. Barr, *Pittsburgh Gazette* (June 30, 1787).

"Notes on the Observations of William Findley," *Pittsburgh Gazette* (August 3, 1787).

"Narrative of the Transactions of the Late Session of Assembly, So Far as They Respect the System of Confederate Government, Proposed by the General Convention of the States at Philadelphia," *Pittsburgh Gazette* (October 27, 1787).

"Queries to the Assemblyman," *Pittsburgh Gazette* (November 3, 1787).

"On the Running Away of the Nineteen Members of the Assembly from the House, When It Was Proposed to Call a Convention to Consider the New System of Congressional Government; and on the Apology Made by Them in Their Address. A Hudibrastic," *Pittsburgh Gazette* (November 3, 10, 1787).

"On the Popularity of . . . [William Findley]," *Pittsburgh Gazette* (December 1, 1787).

"A Memoir to the American Philosophical Society" (1787), in *Gazette Publications*, Carlisle, 1806, pp. 256-64.

"Address and Reasons of Dissent of the Minority of the Convention of the State of Pennsylvania to their Constituents," *Pittsburgh Gazette* (January 26, 1788).

"Cursory Remarks on the Federal Constitution," *Pittsburgh Gazette* (March 1 and 15, 1788).

"Apology for the Dissentients in the State Constitution," *Pittsburgh Gazette* (March 7, 1788).

"Sermons in Favor of the Federal Constitution," *Pittsburgh Gazette* (March 22, 29 and April 5, 12, 1788).

"A Sermon on Village Slander," *Pittsburgh Gazette* (March 29, June 20, 1788).

"On the Road Bill," *Pittsburgh Gazette* (April 26, May 3, 10, 17, 1788).

"To the Dissenting Assemblyman by an Assenting Constituent," *Pittsburgh Gazette* (May 10, 1788).

"On the Subject of Calling a Convention," *Pittsburgh Gazette* (May 23, 1788).

Oration on the Federal Constitution, *Pittsburgh Gazette* (June 28, 1788).

"Sermon on the Duel," *Pittsburgh Gazette* (June 13, 1789).

"Thoughts on the Present Indian War," *National Gazette* (February 2, 6, 1792).

Selected Bibliography

"Thoughts on the Excise Law, So Far as It Respects the Western Country," *National Gazette* (February 9, 1792).

"Modern Chevalier" (c. 1790), in *Gazette Publications*, 1806, pp. 311 ff.

Modern Chivalry: Containing the Adventures of Captain John Farrago, and Teague O'Regan, His Servant. Vols. I, II. Philadelphia: John M'Culloch, 1792.

Modern Chivalry. Vol. III. Pittsburgh: John Scull, 1793.

"Louis Capet Lost his Caput," *National Gazette* (April 20, 1793).

"Open Letter to President Washington Criticizing his Neutrality Proclamation," *National Gazette* (May 15, 1793).

Oration of July 4, 1793, *National Gazette* (July 27, 1793).

Discussion of the "proposition of Genet" and the President's attitude toward it, *Pittsburgh Gazette* (January 18, 1794).

Open letter to the militia pleading for justice to himself, *Pittsburgh Gazette* (November 8, 1794).

Incidents of the Insurrection in the Western Parts of Pennsylvania in the Year 1794. Philadelphia: John M'Culloch, 1795.

Modern Chivalry, Vol. IV. Philadelphia: John M'Culloch, 1797.

"Sketch of the Ground of My Opposition to the Election of John Woods as a Representative in Congress," *Pittsburgh Gazette* (September 29, 1798).

"To the Citizens of Greene, Washington, and Allegheny Counties," *Pittsburgh Gazette* (September 1, 1798).

Article regarding a new newspaper in Pittsburgh, *Pittsburgh Gazette* (December 7, 1799).

Open letter to Judge Alexander Addison, *Tree of Liberty* (November 15, 1800).

"On the Blackguard Writers in *Scull's Gazette* in the Course of the Summer," *Tree of Liberty* (November 22, 1800).

"Scots Poems addressed to David Bruce," in *Poems of the Scots-Irishman*. Washington, Pa.: John Colerick, 1801; and *Gazette Publications*, 1806.

"Jefferson: In Imitation of Virgil's Pollio," *Tree of Liberty* (January 25, 1801).

"To the Scots-Irishman," *Tree of Liberty* (February 14, 1801).

"On the Means of Reconciling Parties," *Tree of Liberty* (June 20 and July 11, 1801).

"A Dogrel Said to Be by Auld Brackie on the Scots-Irishman," *Tree of Liberty* (June 20, 1801).

Modern Chivalry, Part I, Vols. I, II. Philadelphia: J. Conrad, 1804.

Modern Chivalry, Part II, Vol. I. Carlisle, Pa.: A. Loudon, 1804.

Modern Chivalry, Part II, Vol. II. Carlisle: Archibald Loudon, 1805.

"The Standard of Liberty," *Freeman's Journal* (July 16, 17, 18, 19, 1805).

"Ironical Reasons for a New Governor and Constitution," *Freeman's Journal* (July 29, 1805).

"Amicus Amicorum, or a Friend of the Friends of the People," *Freeman's Journal* (July 31 and August 1, 1805).

"An Address to the Federalists," *Freeman's Journal* (August 3 and 5, 1805).

Gazette Publications. Carlisle: Alexander & Phillips, 1806.

The Spirit of the Public Journals, or Beauties of American Newspapers, for 1805, ed. Carlisle: Geo. Dobbin & Murphy, 1806.

Modern Chivalry, Part I, Vols. III, IV. Carlisle, Pa.: Alexander and Phillips, 1807.

"The Trial of Mamachtaga" and "The Lone Indian," in Archibald Loudon's *Indian Narratives*. Carlisle: A. Loudon, 1808.

"On the Conclusiveness of a Foreign Court of Admirality," *Poulson's Advertizer* (January 6, 1808).

Considerations of Jurisprudence of the State of Pennsylvania. Philadelphia, 1808.

"An Epistle to Walter Scott. Written in Pittsburgh During Sitting of the Term, by H. H. Brackenridge, on Reading 'The Lady of the Lake'— Taken Up by Chance," Pittsburgh: Franklin Head Printing-office, 1811.

Law Miscellanies. Philadelphia: P. Byrne, 1814.

Modern Chivalry, revised edition. Philadelphia and Richmond: Johnson and Warner, 1815.

Modern Chivalry, revised edition. Pittsburgh: R. Patterson and Lambdin, 1819.

Modern Chivalry, Part I. Wilmington, Del.: Kollock and Metz, 1825.

Modern Chivalry, Part I. Philadelphia: Carey and Hart, 1846.

Modern Chivalry, Part I. Philadelphia: Getz and Buck, 1851 .

Modern Chivalry, Part I. Philadelphia: Carey and Hart, 1856.

Modern Chivalry, ed. ERNEST BRENECKE. New York: Greenberg (The Rogues Bookshelf), 1926.

Modern Chivalry, ed. CLAUDE M. NEWLIN. New York: American Book Company, 1937.

Modern Chivalry, ed. LEWIS LEARY. New York: Twayne Publishers, 1965.

SECONDARY SOURCES

ADAMS, HENRY. *History of the United States of America*. Vol. I. New York: Charles Scribner's Sons, 1889-1901. The significance of Brackenridge as early frontier writer.

AGNEW, HENRY. *Sketches of Prominent Lawyers of the Allegheny County Bar of the Last Century and Earlier Years of This*. Philadelphia: n.p., 1889. Physical description and a view of Brackenridge at the bar of justice.

ANDREWS, CUTLER J. "The Pittsburgh Gazette—a Pioneer Newspaper," *Western Pennsylvania Historical Magazine*, XV (November, 1932), 293-307. The role of Brackenridge in establishing the first newspaper west of the Alleghenies.

BALDWIN, LELAND D. *Pittsburgh: The Story of a City* (Pittsburgh: University of Pittsburgh Press, 1938). Brackenridge as civic leader, innovator of cultural organizations, and as frontier oddity.

BINNEY, HORACE. *Reports of Cases Adjudged in the Supreme Court of Pennsylvania*. 6 vols. Philadelphia: Moses Thomas, 1809-1815. Brackenridge as Supreme Court Justice with feet on the bench.

BRACKENRIDGE, HENRY MARIE. "Biographical Notice of H. H. Brackenridge. Late of the Supreme Court of Pennsylvania," *Southern Literary Messenger*, VIII (January, 1842), 1-19. A son's biographical eulogy.

Selected Bibliography

——. *History of the Western Insurrection in Western Pennsylvania, Commonly Called the Whiskey Insurrection. 1794.* Pittsburgh: Printed by W. S. Haven, 1859. According to his son's view, Brackenridge adhered to a role of moderator.

——. *Recollection of Persons and Places in the West.* Philadelphia: J. Kay, Jun., and Brother. A stern and distant father and disciplinarian.

Bradford Papers. Historical Society of Pennsylvania (Manuscript Department), Philadelphia. Manuscripts of early work at Princeton.

BROWN, DAVID PAUL. *The Forum, or Forty Years Full Practice at the Philadelphia Bar.* Vol. I, Philadelphia: R. H. Small, 1856. Intimate view of Brackenridge as Supreme Court Justice.

BRUCE, DAVID. *Poems Chiefly in the Scottish Dialect, Originally Written Under the Signature of the Scot-Irishman, by a Native of Scotland.* Washington, Pennsylvania: John Colerick, 1801. Dialect poems inspired by Brackenridge, a fellow Scotsman of opposite political persuasion.

COBBETT, WILLIAM. *Porcupine's Works,* I. London: Printed for Cobbett and Morgan, 1801. Critical admiration for *Incidents of the Insurrection* as intense and realistic literature.

CONNERS, MARTHA. "Hugh Henry Brackenridge at Princeton University, 1768-1771," *Western Pennsylvania Historical Magazine,* X (July, 1927), 146-62. Curriculum, literary efforts, friendships.

COWIE, ALEXANDER. *The Rise of the American Novel.* New York: American Book Co., 1948. Appraisal of *Modern Chivalry* and its place in American literature.

CRAIG, NEVILLE B. *Exposure of a few of the Many Misstatements in H. M. Brackenridge's History of the Whiskey Insurrection.* Pittsburgh: J. S. Davison, 1859. Effort to destroy Brackenridge's account of his role in the Insurrection as reinforced by his son's narrative.

EDEL, WILLIAM W. *Bulwark of Liberty.* Carlisle, Pennsylvania: Dickinson College, 1950. Customary view of Brackenridge as wooly Western character with unusual talents and achievements.

FIELD, ALSTON G. "The Press in Western Pennsylvania to 1812," *Western Pennsylvania Historical Magazine,* XX (December, 1937), 231-64. Account of *Pittsburgh Gazette* and Brackenridge's role in forming it.

FINDLEY, WILLIAM. *History of the Insurrection in the Four Western Counties of Pennsylvania,* Philadelphia: Printed by Samuel Harrison Smith, 1796. Anti-Brackenridge account of the Insurrection.

FLEMING, GEORGE T. "Early Social Life in Pittsburgh," *Gazette Times,* February 15, 1920. The social milieu of Pittsburgh in the days of Brackenridge.

HAVILAND, THOMAS P. "Hugh Henry Brackenridge and Milton's 'Piedmontese' Sonnet," *Notes and Queries,* CLXXVI (April 8, 1939), 243-44. Comparison of verse shows Brackenridge's heavy reliance on Milton.

HAVILAND, T. P. "The Miltonic Quality of Brackenridge's 'Poem on Divine Revelation,'" *PMLA,* LVI (June, 1941), 588-92.

HEISER, M. F. "The Decline of Neo-Classicism: 1801-1848," *Transitions in American Literary History,* ed. HARRY HAYDEN CLARK. Durham, North Carolina: Duke University Press, 1953. Brackenridge as the most typical neo-classicist in North America.

HENRICKSON, JOHN R. "The Influence of Don Quixote on *Modern Chivalry*." Ph.D. dissertation, Florida State University, 1959. How Brackenridge used Cervantes' picaresque novel.

HOLLIDAY, CARL. *Wit and Humor of Colonial Days*. Philadelphia: J. B. Lippincott Company, 1912. Account of Brackenridge family arriving and settling in America.

HOWARD, LEON. "The Influence of Milton on Colonial Poetry," *The Huntington Library Bulletin*, No. 9 (April, 1936), 63-89. Brackenridge verse is typical.

Journals of the House of Representatives of the Commonwealth of Pennsylvania. Lancaster, 1803-1804. Speeches of Brackenridge as representative of the Western country.

KILLIKELLY, SARAH H. *The History of Pittsburgh*. Pittsburgh: B. C. & Gordon Montgomery Co., 1906. Brackenridge's role in starting a library for inhabitants of Pittsburgh.

LEARY, LEWIS. "Father Bombo's Pilgrimage," *Pennsylvania Magazine of History and Biography*, LXVI (October, 1942), 459-78. Emphasis on authorship of Freneau.

"The Library," *Pennsylvania Magazine*, LXXI (1947), 44-67. Account of hatred New Jersey troops felt for Brackenridge as they marched west to suppress the Insurrection.

Literary Examiner, and Western Monthly Review, Pittsburgh, I (May, 1839), 27-29. A note on the high esteem *Modern Chivalry* had reached by 1839.

LOSHE, LILLIE. *The Early American Novel*. New York: The Columbia University Press, 1907. Contribution of *Modern Chivalry* in history of American novel.

LOUDON, ARCHIBALD (ed.). *Selection of Some of the Most Interesting Narratives of Outrages Committed by the Indians in Their Wars with the White People*. Carlisle, Pennsylvania: A. Loudon, 1808. Two Brackenridge accounts of Indians sympathetically rendered are juxtaposed with two narratives of Indian atrocities.

McDOWELL, TREMAINE. "Sensibility in the Eighteenth Century American Novel," *Studies in Philology*, XXIV (July, 1927), 382-402. Sentimental elements in *Modern Chivalry*.

MOORE, FRANK. *American Eloquence*. Philadelphia: D. Appleton and Company, 1857. Republication of Brackenridge oratory.

NEWLIN, CLAUDE M. *The Life and Writings of Hugh Henry Brackenridge*. Princeton: Princeton University Press, 1932. The only full-scale biography of Brackenridge; not an evaluation of his work.

————— (ed.). *Modern Chivalry by Hugh Henry Brackenridge*. New York: American Book Company, 1937. Precise reproduction of entire work.

PARRINGTON, VERNON LOUIS. *Main Currents in American Thought*. I. New York: Harcourt, Brace, 1927. Appreciation of Brackenridge as early frontier writer and democratic influence.

PATTEE, FRED LEWIS (ed.). *The Poems of Philip Freneau: Poet of the American Revolution*. I. Princeton: Princeton Historical Association, 1902. Appraisal of Brackenridge as fiction writer, publisher of *United States Magazine*, and poet.

PAULDING, JAMES KIRKE. *Life of Washington*, II. New York: Harper & Brothers, 1845. Admiration of Brackenridge as satirist.

Pittsburgh Gazette (1786-1804). Many articles by Brackenridge and many more about him, mostly pejorative.

POPE, JOHN. *A Tour Through the Southern and Western Territories of the United States of North America; the Spanish Dominions on the River Mississippi, and the Floridas; the Countries of the Creek Nations; and Many Uninhabited Parts.* Richmond: by J. Dixon, for his author, 1792. Entertaining account of Brackenridge's second marriage.

QUINN, ARTHUR HOBSON. *American Fiction.* New York: D. Appleton-Century Company, 1936. Historical treatment of Brackenridge as novelist.

————. *A History of the American Drama from the Beginning to the Civil War.* New York: Harper & Brothers, 1923. Praise of Brackenridge as best playwright of Revolution.

RICHARDSON, L. N. *History of Early American Magazines, 1740-1789*, New York: T. Nelson and Sons, 1931. Fullest account of *United States Magazine.*

SPILLER, ROBERT E., *et al.* (eds.). *Literary History of the United States.* I. New York: Macmillan, 1948. Summary treatment of *Modern Chivalry.*

STARRETT, AGNES LYNCH. *Through One Hundred and Fifty Years: The University of Pittsburgh.* Pittsburgh: University of Pittsburgh Press, 1937. Brackenridge's role in founding first academy west of the mountains.

Tree of Liberty, Pittsburgh (1800-1804). Brackenridge feuds with the *Pittsburgh Gazette* and Federalists.

TRENT, WILLIAM PETERFIELD, *et al.* (eds.). *The Cambridge History of American Literature.* I. New York: Macmillan, 1933. Summary of *Modern Chivalry.*

TYLER, MOSES COIT. *The Literary History of the American Revolution.* II. New York: G. P. Putnam's Sons, 1897. Fullest appreciation of Brackenridge's work, including sermons, plays, fiction.

WHITE, J. W. F. "The Judiciary of Allegheny Court," *Pennsylvania Magazine*, VII (1883), 148-93. Account of the defense of the Indian Mamachtaga.

Index

Index